PERSPECTIVES

PRE-INTERMEDIATE

Lewis **LANSFORD**

Daniel **BARBER**

Amanda **JEFFRIES**

**NATIONAL
GEOGRAPHIC**

L E A R N I N G

Australia · Brazil · Mexico · Singapore · United Kingdom · United States

Perspectives teaches learners to think critically and to develop the language skills they need to find their own voice in English. The carefully guided language lessons, real-world stories and TED Talks motivate learners to think creatively and communicate effectively.

In *Perspectives*, learners develop:

● AN OPEN MIND

Every unit explores one idea from different perspectives, giving learners opportunities for practising language as they look at the world in new ways.

• A CRITICAL EYE

Students learn the critical thinking skills and strategies they need to evaluate new information and develop their own opinions and ideas to share.

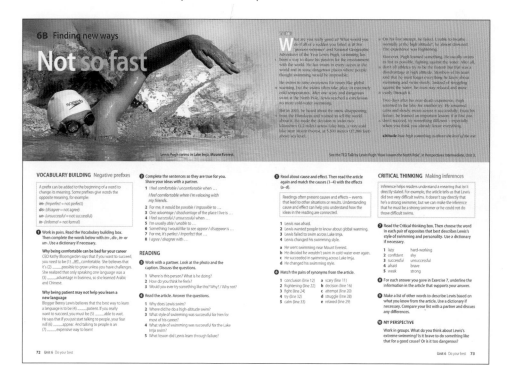

• A CLEAR VOICE

Students respond to the unit theme and express their own ideas confidently in English.

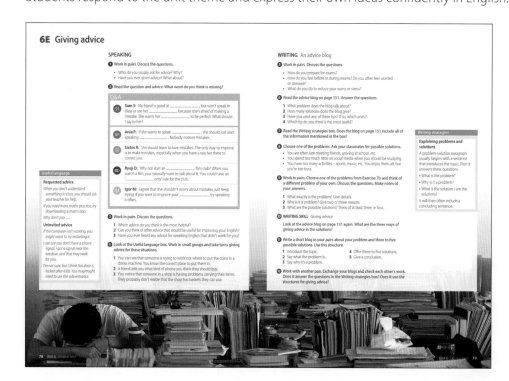

CONTENTS

GRAMMAR	TEDTALKS		SPEAKING	WRITING
Verb patterns: verb + -ing or infinitive with to	**Half a million secrets**	**FRANK WARREN** Frank Warren's idea worth spreading is that sharing secrets can help us connect with others and know ourselves better. **Authentic listening skills** Word stress **Critical thinking** Identifying the main idea	Talking about likes and dislikes	An introductory postcard **Writing skill** Using informal language
Past continuous **Pronunciation** -ing in fast speech	**Magical houses, made of bamboo**	**ELORA HARDY** Elora Hardy's idea worth spreading is that bamboo is an incredibly adaptable and strong building material that pushes the boundaries of what we can create with sustainable materials. **Authentic listening skills** Listening for gist	Giving reasons	A description **Writing skill** Using adjectives
Phrasal verbs	**The amazing story of the man who gave us modern pain relief**	**LATIF NASSER** Latif Nasser's idea worth spreading is that pain is a testament to a fully lived life, an essential part of the human experience that all of us – including doctors – must acknowledge and deal with. **Authentic listening skills** Collaborative listening	Giving opinions, disagreeing and conceding a point	An opinion essay **Writing skill** Organizing points in an essay
Comparative forms (as … as, too, enough, so, such)	**Don't eat the marshmallow!**	**JOACHIM DE POSADA** Joachim de Posada's idea worth spreading is that children who pass the 'marshmallow test' could potentially be more successful in life since the results show signs of patience and self-discipline. **Authentic listening skills** English speakers with accents	Asking about opinions, making comparisons, making a decision	An enquiry email **Writing skill** Using polite expressions
Present perfect with for, since, already, just and yet	**Why we laugh**	**SOPHIE SCOTT** Sophie Scott's idea worth spreading is that laughter is an ancient behaviour that we use to benefit ourselves and others in complex and surprising ways. **Authentic listening skills** Dealing with fast speech **Critical thinking** Recognize supporting evidence	Talking about availability, accepting and saying no to an invitation	Informal invitations and replies **Writing skill** Politely making and replying to invitations

CONTENTS

GRAMMAR	TEDTALKS		SPEAKING	WRITING
Zero conditional **Pronunciation** Conditional intonation	 **Teach girls bravery, not perfection**	**RESHMA SAUJANI** Reshma Saujani's idea worth spreading is that we should teach girls, and all children, that we succeed not by aiming for perfection, but by knowing that we all make mistakes and being brave enough to try anyway. **Authentic listening skills** Contrast	Giving advice	An advice blog **Writing skill** Giving advice
First conditional	 **The global food waste scandal**	**TRISTRAM STUART** Tristram Stuart's idea worth spreading is that good, fresh food is being wasted on a colossal scale – and that we have the power to stop this tragic waste of resources. **Authentic listening skills** Prediction **Critical thinking** Supporting evidence	Planning a meal: making suggestions, describing food, and making decisions	A restaurant review **Writing skill** Writing a review
Defining relative clauses	 **Our campaign to ban plastic bags in Bali**	**MELATI AND ISABEL WIJSEN** The Wijsens' idea worth spreading is that when kids apply their energy and perseverance to improve the world, they can bring about amazing changes. **Authentic listening skills** Content words **Critical thinking** A speaker's authority	How to persuade	A persuasive blog post **Writing skill** Using persuasive language
Reported speech	 **The surprising thing I learned sailing solo around the world**	**DAME ELLEN MACARTHUR** Ellen MacArthur's idea worth spreading is that we live in a world of infinite possibilities, but finite resources – and this requires creative thinking about our global economy and our individual lifestyles. **Authentic listening skills** Weak forms	Talking about careers, skills and interests **Pronunciation** Wh- question intonation	A formal email **Writing skill** Indirect questions
The passive with *by* + agent	 **How to control someone else's arm with your brain**	**GREG GAGE** Greg Gage's idea worth spreading is that we can use DIY neuroscience equipment to help more people understand and participate in brain science. **Authentic listening skills** Reduced forms **Critical thinking** Analyze how a message is delivered	Talking about pros and cons: looking at two sides in an argument	A formal letter of suggestion **Writing skill** Writing politely

Marta (main photo) and Emma (inset photo) are twins. Twins can have the same eyes and the same colour hair, but one may be shy, while the other loves meeting new people.

IN THIS UNIT YOU

- learn about occupations, interests and descriptions

- talk about yourself and others

- read about how people show emotions

- watch a TED Talk about people's secrets

- speak and write about what you like to do

1A He's really into music

VOCABULARY Personality

1 MY PERSPECTIVE

Work in pairs. Discuss the questions.

1 Look at the photo and read the caption. Are you like any members of your family?
2 Circle two or three of these words to describe yourself.

cool	friendly	funny	happy	honest	intelligent
kind	loud	nasty	nice	popular	shy

3 Think of two or three words that other people might use to describe you.
4 Were your answers to questions 2 and 3 the same or different? Why?

2 Match the pairs of words that have a similar meaning. Use a dictionary if necessary. Then think of someone you know that you can describe with each pair of words.

1 smart   a relaxed
2 calm   b nice
3 helpful   c intelligent
4 cheerful   d kind

3 Choose the correct option to complete each sentence.

1 I'm *active / lazy* at the weekend. I usually do some sport and go out with my friends.
2 He's *confident / nervous* about giving presentations because he doesn't like making mistakes.
3 She's very *sociable / shy* and has a lot of friends.
4 Our coach is *serious / easy-going* and lets us listen to music before basketball practice.
5 Kenji is very *hard-working / talented*. He isn't the best, but he really wants to succeed.
6 Luis is really *loud / quiet*. You always know when he's in a room!
7 Maria's very *honest / funny* – she always makes her classmates laugh.
8 Samir usually helps his little sister with her homework. He's very *nasty / kind*.

4 Work in pairs. Take turns to describe people in your class, but don't say their names. Can your partner guess who you're talking about?

She's calm, helpful and cheerful.
  Is it Li?

No. She's also very active – but a little bit shy.
  Oh, is it Ana?

5 Work in pairs. Think of a famous person together. Then, working separately, each make a list of words to describe this person. Use a dictionary if necessary. Then compare your lists. Did you use any of the same words? Do you agree with your partner's description? Why? / Why not?

6 Work with the same partner. Make one list for your person using all the words you agree on. Read your list from Exercise 5 to the class. Can the class guess your person?

LISTENING

7 Look at the picture and caption. Answer the questions.

1 What do you think DJ Spooky means by 'We're all nature'?
- **a** We are made of trees.
- **b** We are part of the planet.
- **c** We are animals.

2 What type of music do you think DJ Spooky makes?
- **a** hip-hop
- **b** classical
- **c** rock

3 What types of music do you enjoy? Hip-hop? Rock? Pop? Jazz? Some other kind?

8 Listen to the conversation between two students meeting for the first time at a party. Write B (Bruno) or A (Anna). 🎧 **2**

Who …
1 listens to the school radio station?
2 listens to DJ Spooky?
3 plays an instrument?
4 plays sports?
5 is looking for new music?

9 Are the sentences true (T), false (F), or is the information not given (NG)? Listen again to check your answers. 🎧 **2**

1 Bruno and Anna like the music at the party.
2 Bruno and Anna both like hip-hop and rock.
3 Anna plays the guitar.
4 DJ Spooky mixes many styles of music.
5 DJ Spooky has a serious personality.
6 Anna likes DJ Spooky's music.

10 Work in pairs. Practise asking and answering questions about interests.

Are you into music / sports / books?

   Yes, I am. / No, not really.

What kind of music / sports / books do you like?

   I'm into rock / baseball / science fiction.

GRAMMAR Present simple and present continuous

11 Look at the sentences in the Grammar box. Underline the verb in each one.

Present simple and present continuous

Present simple

They play really good music.

I play the guitar – a little bit.

Present continuous

They're playing really good music.

I'm looking for some new music to listen to.

12 Answer the questions about the sentences in the Grammar box.

1 Which tense describes an activity happening now or around now?
2 Which tense describes something that happens regularly or all the time?
3 How do we form the present continuous?

Check your answers on page 128. Do Exercises 1–4.

13 Complete the information about DJ Spooky. Use the present simple of the verbs in brackets.

DJ Spooky's real name (1) _____ (be) Paul D Miller. He (2) _____ (live) in New York but he (3) _____ (have) fans all over the world. They (4) _____ (love) his shows – especially the way he (5) _____ (use) music and pictures together. 'I (6) _____ (like) to think of music not just as music, but as information,' he says. 'Art and music and science and technology (7) _____ (not be) separate things.' At his concerts, people (8) _____ (hear) music, (9) _____ (see) pictures of the natural world, and most of all, (10) _____ (learn).

14 Complete the short conversations with the *-ing* form of these verbs.

do	enjoy	live	play	read
sit	stay	study	take	wait

1 A: What are you _____ out there?
   B: We're _____ tennis, but we can't find the ball.

2 A: Why are you _____ in your room?
   B: I'm _____ for a friend to call, but she's late.

3 A: Is your brother _____ a new language at college?
   B: No, he isn't _____ languages any more.

4 A: I'm _____ a book by a Chilean author at the moment.
   B: Oh, are you _____ it?

5 A: Is your sister still _____ with her friends near the college?
   B: No, she isn't. She's _____ in one of the college rooms now. It's much better.

15 Complete the sentences with the present simple or present continuous of the verbs in brackets.

1 My sister usually _____ (watch) TV at night.
2 David _____ (be) from Mexico City.
3 Marta isn't here because she _____ (study) in the library.
4 Our football team _____ (practise) on Saturdays.
5 Be quiet, please. I _____ (try) to use the phone.
6 Mum _____ (make) a chocolate cake. It smells fantastic!
7 Fatima's bringing her guitar this evening. She _____ (play) really well.
8 We want to go to the park, but it _____ (rain) too heavily.

16 Complete the conversation with the present simple or present continuous of the verbs.

be	be	do	go	play	wait	want	work

A: What (1) _____ you _____ right now?
B: I (2) _____ to Ella's house.
A: Who (3) _____ Ella?
B: She (4) _____ a friend from my basketball team. We (5) _____ basketball after school on Tuesdays. (6) _____ you _____ to come?
A: Sorry, I can't. I (7) _____ for Tony because we (8) _____ together on a science project.

17 PRONUNCIATION *-s* verb endings

a Look at the pronunciation box and listen to the examples below it. Write the words in the correct list. 🎧 **3**

> There are three ways to pronounce *-s* at the end of a verb: /s/ as in *gets*, /z/ as in *sings*, or /ɪz/ as in *washes*.

goes	likes	listens	plays	practises
uses	wants	watches	writes	

/s/ *works,*

/z/ *sings,*

/ɪz/ *dances,*

b Listen again to check your answers. 🎧 **3**

18 MY PERSPECTIVE

Work in pairs. Find five things that you like and five different things that your partner likes. Make sentences about them to share with the class. Use these verbs or your own ideas.

- like (music, sports, books)
- watch (TV shows, films)
- want (a pet, a new phone)
- play (guitar, video games)
- go (to the park, shopping)

She plays the guitar, but I play the piano.

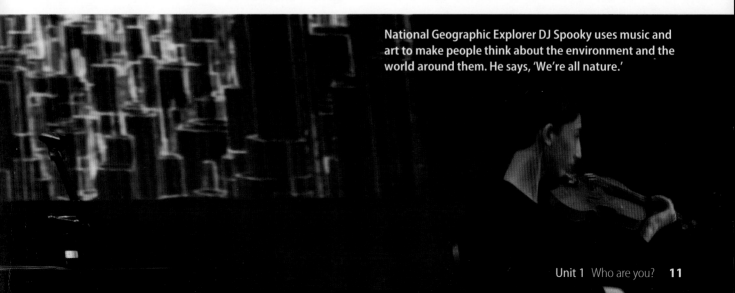

National Geographic Explorer DJ Spooky uses music and art to make people think about the environment and the world around them. He says, 'We're all nature.'

1B How are you feeling?

VOCABULARY BUILDING Adjective complements

Complements follow verbs like *be*, *become*, *look* and *seem*. They are usually adjectives and we often use them to describe emotions.

She **looks nervous**.   I'm **bored**.   You **seem angry**.

1 Look at the table and choose the best words to complete the sentences.

Start to experience an emotion: *become / get*	afraid	angry
Experience an emotion: *feel / be*	bored	excited
	frightened	nervous
Appear to experience an emotion: *look / seem*	upset	worried

1 Are you _afraid/frightened/nervous/worried_ ? Don't worry. The test won't be that bad.
2 I'm getting _excited_ about my holiday next week.
3 They feel _nervous/worried_ about their exams next month.
4 Dan _is/looks/seems_ upset about something, but I don't know what the problem is.
5 The teacher _became/got/was_ angry when everyone was late.
6 You _seem/look_ nervous about the test, but I'm sure you'll do well.

2 Work in pairs. Pick three of the emotions in Exercise 1. Tell a partner about a time you felt each one.

READING

3 Read about previewing a text. Preview the article and answer the questions.

Before you read a text, preview it. This will help you understand what it's about before you read it carefully.

- Look at the title. What is the text probably about? _feelings_
- Look at any pictures. What do they tell you about the text?
- Read the first and last paragraph. What are the main ideas?

4 Read the article. Match each paragraph with one of the ideas (a–e).

a There are four types of feelings. 2 (10-11)
b Animals experience emotions. 4 (33-34)
c Some animals understand human feelings. 3 (21-22)
d Seeing people is an important part of communication. 5 (48-49)
e Humans experience many different feelings. 1 (4-5)

5 Read the article again. Choose the correct option to complete each sentence.

1 Recent scientific research _b_ the idea that we experience many very different feelings. *para 1*
   a proves   b disagrees with
   c says nothing about
2 According to researchers, feeling nervous is basically the same as being
   a sad.   b angry.   c afraid. *para 2*
3 People everywhere show their emotions
   a on their face.   b in their voice. *para 2*
   c through their words.
4 Researchers found that horses recognize ____ emotions on people's faces. *para 3*
   a four   b three   c two
5 Horses understand people's feelings because
   a horses' brains are like people's brains.
   b they work closely with people. *para 3*
   c people teach them to understand.
6 Carl Safina believes that human and animal emotions are
   a very different.   b similar.
   c impossible to compare. *para 4*
7 According to the article, animals ____ with each other.
   a share their emotions
   b communicate in 'animal language' *para 4*
   c often feel angry
8 Understanding feelings helps us
   a stop feeling angry.
   b control animals. *para 5*
   c communicate.

6 Which of these statements is true, according to the article? Underline the information that explains your answer.

1 Some animals can understand human language.
2 Email isn't a good way to discuss important things. (53-55)
3 We should try to hide our feelings from animals.

7 MY PERSPECTIVE

Work in pairs. Discuss the questions.

- What did you learn from the article?
- Did the article change your thinking about animals and emotions?
- Do you think it's true that we should have some discussions face to face? Why? Give examples.

IT'S WRITTEN ALL OVER YOUR FACE

🎧 4 How are you feeling right now?

Excited? Bored? Worried? Upset? How many possible answers are there? Interested, nervous, relaxed, angry, lonely … the list goes on. We feel so many different
5 things, so feelings can seem very complicated. But recent scientific research actually says this might not be completely true.

Basic feelings

A group of scientists at the University of Glasgow in
10 Scotland say that people only experience four basic feelings: sad, happy, angry and afraid. All of the other feelings we describe are really part of one of the basic four. So if you feel worried or nervous, that's fear. If you're relaxed or excited, that's happiness. If you're
15 bored or lonely, that's sadness. Many scientists also say that people all over the world can see these feelings in the faces of the people around them. In fact, we're so good at it, we can easily understand the feelings on the face of a cartoon.

Try it! Look at the pictures and match each one with a basic feeling – sad, happy, angry, afraid.

THE FOUR BASIC FEELINGS

---

20 Not just for humans

Our faces show our feelings so clearly that even some animals know how we feel. Scientists at the University of Essex in the UK say that horses can identify happy or angry faces and can even recognize these feelings on
25 the faces of strangers. This makes sense because horses live and work closely with humans in many places. They enjoy being with happy people. They also learn to avoid angry people whenever possible. Scientists want to know more. Can we expect animals to
30 recognize other feelings, too? The research continues.

What do animals feel?

It's not just horses that recognize human emotions. Animal expert Carl Safina believes that other animals experience many of the same feelings people have.
35 'They play. They act frightened when there's danger. They relax when things are good,' he says. In his book *Beyond Words: What Animals Think and Feel*, Safina explains that dogs, elephants and even whales* show their feelings and understand the feelings of other
40 animals. He tells the story of a whale who rescued a seal* from danger, and says that elephants love meeting their friends and become very sad when a friend or family member dies. Scientists say that emotions help animals to survive. For example, research shows that
45 animals who don't feel fear don't live for very long.

Face time

Understanding feelings is important. In fact, it's so important that people's faces usually tell others exactly how they feel, and these feelings are often
50 obvious to us. We can use this information to make communication easier, or sometimes to know what other people are thinking or feeling, even when they don't tell us. So, when you need to talk about something important, try to have a face-to-face
55 conversation – or at least a video chat.

whale *a large sea mammal that breathes through the top of its head*
seal *a sea mammal with thick fur and flippers*

Two friends talking on a
bridge in Johor, Malaysia.

1C I expect my friends to understand

GRAMMAR Verb patterns: verb + -ing or infinitive with to

1 Work in pairs. Discuss the following.

- Name two or three things you love doing.
- Name two or three things you hate doing.

2 Look at the Grammar box. Underline the first verb in each sentence. Circle the verb that follows it.

Verbs + -ing or infinitive with to
They enjoy being with happy people.
They also learn to avoid angry people whenever possible.
Scientists want to know more.
Elephants love meeting their friends.

3 Look again at the sentences in the Grammar box. Complete the table with the underlined verbs.

Verbs followed by ...	
the -ing form	to + infinitive
enjoy	learn
love	want

Check your answers on page 128. Do Exercises 5–7.

4 Choose the correct option to complete each sentence. Are any of the sentences true for you?

1 I suggest *talking* / *to talk* to someone when you feel lonely.
2 Whenever I feel happy, I want *sharing* / *to share* it with my friends!
3 I always manage *making* / *to make* myself feel better when I discuss my problems with someone.
4 I can't help *feeling* / *to feel* closer to my friends when I share how I feel with them.
5 My friends and I don't mind *telling* / *to tell* each other about our feelings. It's free entertainment!

5 Complete the text with the verb + -ing or the infinitive with *to*. Sometimes both options are possible.

We can't help (1) _smiling_ (smile) when the people around us smile. And when we see our friends laugh, it makes us want (2) _to laugh_ (laugh), too. It's almost impossible to avoid (3) _sharing_ (share) the feelings of the people around us. But this doesn't stop with being happy, sad, angry or afraid. It affects us physically, too! Our own body temperature actually begins (4) _to drop / dropping_ (drop) when we watch someone put their hand in ice water.

Why are we able to feel the emotions of the people around us? Humans need (5) _to understand_ (understand) each other well because we spend a lot of time working together. When we don't manage (6) _to get on_ (get on), we may start (7) _fighting / to fight_ (fight) – and that's bad for everyone.

6 Complete the short conversations with the correct form of the verbs. Sometimes more than one option is possible.

bother	describe
help	receive
send	share
talk	tell
not tell	write

1 A: I hate _to bother_ you, but can I ask for some advice?
   B: I don't mind _helping_ you, but I can't talk right now. I'm late for class!

2 A: Do you promise _not to tell_ my secret?
   B: I'm not sure! Sometimes I can't help _sharing_ secrets!

3 A: I like _to write / writing_ about my feelings in a notebook.
   B: I don't do that. I prefer _talking to talk_ to someone face-to-face.

4 A: I plan _to send_ you a postcard from my holiday.
   B: Oh, thanks. I love _to receive / receiving_ postcards.

5 A: My sister has agreed _to describe_ everything that happens at the concert.
   B: Oh, good. Do you promise _to tell_ me everything too?

7 Complete the sentences with true information about yourself. Use verb + -ing and infinitives with to.

1 I like _____ at the weekend.
   I like riding my bike at the weekend.
2 I want _____ next summer.
3 I usually avoid _____ .
4 I hope _____ before I'm 20 years old.
5 I need _____ for school.

8 Work in pairs. Take turns to ask and answer questions about Exercise 7. Use the correct form of *do* in the questions.

A: *What do you like doing at the weekend?*
B: *I like …*
A: *What do you want to do next summer?*
B: *I want …*

9 CHOOSE

1 Ask questions to find other people in the class who are similar to you.

   Do you like riding your bike at the weekend?
       Yes, I do.
   Do you avoid being late for school?
       Of course! But I'm sometimes late anyway.

2 Report back to the class about what you learned about your partner in Exercise 8.

   Majid Ilikes watching films at the weekend.

3 Write a paragraph comparing you and your partner using the information you learned in Exercise 8.

A family laughs on a roller coaster.

> **❝ Secrets can take many forms. They can be shocking or silly or soulful. They can connect us to our deepest humanity or with people we'll never meet again. ❞**
>
> **FRANK WARREN**

Read about Frank Warren and get ready to watch his TED Talk. ▶ **1.0**

AUTHENTIC LISTENING SKILLS

Word stress

In English, words with two or more syllables have the main stress on one of the syllables. Learning the pronunciation of words and where the stress is will help you recognize them when they're being said.

1 Read the Authentic listening skills box. Listen to the words from the TED Talk and underline the syllables that are stressed. 🎧 **5**

1 collect   3 girlfriend   5 advertisement   7 instructions
2 received   4 stranger   6 memory   8 collection

2 Now listen to two extracts from the talk. Notice the stressed syllables in the first extract. Underline the stressed syllables in the second extract. 🎧 **6**

1 Hi, my name is Frank, and I co<u>llect</u> <u>se</u>crets. It all <u>star</u>ted with a <u>cra</u>zy <u>i</u>dea in No<u>vem</u>ber of two <u>thou</u>sand and four.
2 I printed up three thousand self-addressed postcards, just like this. They were blank on one side, and on the other side I listed some simple instructions.

WATCH

3 Watch Part 1 of the talk. Choose the correct option to complete each sentence. ▶ **1.1**

1 Frank gave the postcards to *strangers* / *friends*.
2 The idea *made people angry* / *became very popular*.
3 People from *the US* / *many different countries* sent postcards to Frank.
4 The green postcard was *a little sad* / *very funny*.

4 Complete the sentences. Then watch Part 2 of the talk and check your answers. ▶ **1.2**

cat	email	ending
postcard	ring	website

1 The man's postcard had a picture of a _cat_ and a ring.
2 The man said he wanted to give the _ring_ to the woman.
3 Frank put the _postcard_ on his website.
4 A little while later, Frank received a very happy _email_ from the man.
5 The man and the woman looked at Frank's _website_ together.
6 The story had a happy _ending_ because the woman said yes.

5 Watch Part 3 of the talk. Which ideas does Frank Warren discuss? Tick (√) the ones he mentions. ▶ **1.3**   *1, 3 + 5*

1 The website IFoundYourCamera helps people find lost cameras.
2 Many people feel unhappy when they see their pictures on the website.
3 IFoundYourCamera shows that people want to help other people.
4 The woman in the picture found another person's camera.
5 The man, woman and child in the picture are very happy now.

That Saturday when you wondered
where I was, well,
I was getting your ring.
It's in my pocket right now.

TEDTALKS

6 VOCABULARY IN CONTEXT

a Watch the clips from the talk. Choose the correct meaning of the words and phrases. ▶ 1.4

b Complete the sentences with your own ideas. Then discuss them with a partner.

1 I sometimes *struggle* when … *try with difficulty*
2 My favourite *image* is … *picture*
3 When I need to feel *calm*, I … *relaxed*
4 One time I experienced a *language barrier* when …
communication problem

7 Frank says that secrets can be shocking or silly or soulful. Write a couple of sentences sharing a silly secret about yourself. Choose something that you don't mind telling the whole class.

I always cry at the end of Stars Wars *movies. I try to hide it from my friends and family, but every time I watch one, I cry.*

8 Work in groups. Share your answers to Exercise 7.

CRITICAL THINKING Identifying the main idea

9 Read the Critical thinking box. Then work in pairs. Say what you think the main idea of the talk is.

> Usually a talk contains one main idea, but it isn't always stated directly. You have to think about how all the parts of the talk work together to create a message.

10 Read the statements. Which person do you think correctly identifies the talk's main idea? Why? How are the ones you didn't choose wrong?

1 Frank is showing us that we should have secrets that we never tell. Telling too much information about ourselves can cause real problems.
2 Frank is saying that when we see other people's secrets, we understand that everyone is human – everyone feels the same feelings. This can help us be kind to ourselves and to other people.
3 Frank thinks that writing postcards is a good way to share information. He says that people are honest when they send postcards.

11 MY PERSPECTIVE

Frank talks about the kindness of strangers. Does he think people are generally kind or generally unkind? How do you know? Do you agree with him?

CHALLENGE

Matty's website uses the kindness of strangers to help people find lost cameras and photographs. Can you think of other ways that people help strangers? Write down three ideas and share them with a partner.

People sometimes give directions to strangers who visit their city.

1E What are you into?

SPEAKING

1 MY PERSPECTIVE

Work in pairs. Discuss the questions.

- When you meet someone new, what information do you usually learn about them?
- What are you interested in knowing about other people?
- What do you want them to know or not know about you?

2 Look at the photo and caption below. What do you think these mailboxes say about the people they belong to?

3 Listen to the conversation. Tick (√) the topics the people talk about. 🎧 7

baseball   hiking   football   tennis   running

4 Listen again. Write the missing information in the profiles. 🎧 7

Name: Juan	Name: Becky
Doesn't like: (1) *playing team sports*	Loves: (4)
Doesn't mind: (2)	Best thing about it: (5)
Likes: (3)	Doesn't like: (6)
Favourite place: *the Black Mountains*	Doesn't mind: (7)

5 Make some notes about your own interests. Think about sports, music, hobbies or anything else you like doing.

I like:

Best thing about it:

I don't mind:

I can't stand:

6 Work in pairs. Use your notes above and the expressions in the Useful language box to ask and answer questions about likes and dislikes.

Useful language

Talking about likes and dislikes

Are you into … ?
Do you have a favourite … ?
What do you think of … ?
I'm really into …
I love to …
I'm not that interested in …
I don't mind …
I can't stand …
That's cool! / Really? / Wow!

People express themselves in many ways, including with mailboxes!

WRITING   An introductory postcard

7 Work in pairs. Imagine you are going to write a postcard to a student your age in another country. Think of five pieces of information you would give or topics you would write about to introduce yourself.

8 Read the postcard on page 149 from a student in Spain to a student in Vietnam. Do you think the boys already know each other? Explain your answer.

9 What information does the card give about the sender?

an interesting personal fact	name
hobbies and interests	home town
description of personality	favourite foods
favourite music	something his friends think
favourite school subjects	things he would like to know about Thanh

10 **WRITING SKILL**   Using informal language

a When we write to a friend or someone of our own age, we usually use informal language. Find examples of the following in the postcard.
   1 an informal greeting
   2 contractions
   3 informal vocabulary and expressions
   4 informal questions
   5 an informal ending

b Work in pairs. Think of at least one other example of 1–5 in Exercise 10a.

11 Using your notes from Exercise 7 and the expressions in the Useful language box, write a postcard introducing yourself and asking a couple of questions.

12 Work in pairs. Exchange your postcards. Check each other's work. Does it use the language from the Useful language box correctly and is it informal enough?

2 Where the heart is

TED speaker, Elora Hardy, designs houses using local bamboo in Bali, Indonesia.

2A Different places

VOCABULARY Describing where you live

1 Look at the inside of the house. What things do you see?

stairs	a refrigerator	a sofa
a window	a table	a door
a chair	art/decorations	a light

2 Work in pairs. Look at the photo. Answer the questions.

1 What do you think living in a house like this is like?
2 Would you like to live in a house like this? Why?

3 Complete the city descriptions with the words in the boxes.

| business | lively | old-fashioned | residential | shopping district | walkable |

A new city: Songdo, South Korea

Songdo International Business District is a 'planned' city in South Korea. It includes a (1) __business__ area where companies like Samsung have offices, a (2) _____ with shops and restaurants, and also (3) _____ areas where people live. This includes a skate park and a lake with boats to hire. There's also a (4) _____ and exciting entertainment area, with a concert hall, an arts centre and cinemas. Everywhere in the city is (5) _____ , so people don't need to use their cars much. Bikes are very popular, too. None of the buildings in the city is (6) _____ because the city is only a few years old.

| crowded | historic | modern | rural | suburban | traditional | urban |

An ancient city: Mexico City

Mexico City is about seven hundred years old. The city centre feels very busy and (7) __urban__ , with busy shopping streets which sometimes get very (8) _____ . However, Chapultepec Park, in the middle of the city, is the largest city park in Latin America. It has an amusement park, a swimming pool and an old castle. There aren't many (9) _____ buildings in the (10) _____ city centre. Construction began in the 1500s, so many buildings are old and (11) _____ . There are, however, modern office buildings in Santa Fe, the city's business district. And there are homes and apartment buildings in the more quiet (12) _____ areas, which grew around the city centre in recent times. There are also many beautiful (13) _____ areas – areas without buildings – near Mexico City, like Desierto de los Leones National Park, which is actually within the city limits.

4 MY PERSPECTIVE

Work in pairs. Answer the questions.

1 Are there cities like Songdo or Mexico City in your country? How are they similar?
2 Would you prefer to live in an urban, suburban or rural area? Why? Consider:
   • shops and restaurants
   • green spaces / parks
   • transport
   • entertainment (cinemas, arts, parks)
   • living in a house or an apartment

LISTENING

5 Listen to the news report about living in Vienna, Austria. Choose the correct words to complete the sentences. 🎧 **8**

1 Vienna is one of the world's most *pleasant / expensive* cities.
2 The boy lives in a *modern / historic* area near the city centre.
3 He says that people in New York pay *more / less* to go out with friends.
4 The girl says that the *underground is / restaurants are* open 24 hours.
5 She *lives / works* in the suburbs.
6 She says the suburbs *are / aren't* boring.

6 Work in pairs. Discuss the questions.

- Would you rather live in Vienna, Songdo or Mexico City? Why?
- Nearly half of the world lives in rural areas. What are the pros (good things) about living in a rural area?
- What are the cons (bad things) about living in a rural area?
- Look at the photo of the container house. Do you think the people you listened to would like to live there? Would a house like this fit in your town or city?

GRAMMAR Past simple

7 Work in pairs. Answer the questions from the news report about Vienna. Listen again to check your answers. 🎧 **8**

1 When did the boy's family move to Vienna?
2 Why did they move to Vienna?
3 Where did they stay when they first arrived?
4 Why did the girl's family move to the suburbs*?

suburb *a quiet area just outside of a city*

Past simple
*We **moved** here five years ago.*
*I **didn't like** it at first.*
***Did** you **meet** new friends? Yes, I **did**. I **met** a lot of people.*
*Where **did** you **live** when you were a child? I **lived** in Madrid.*

8 Look at the Grammar box. Match the two parts of the sentences to make rules about the past simple. (Two sentences have the same ending.)

1 For affirmative statements about the past,
2 For negative statements about the past,
3 For questions about the past,
4 We use the past simple to talk about

a we use the past form of *do* and the infinitive.
b actions completed before now.
c the verb shows the past tense.

Check your answers on page 130. Do Exercises 1–5.

In some places, like London, England, entire neighbourhoods are made of shipping containers.

9 We add -(e)d to the infinitive to make the past simple of regular verbs, but many common verbs are irregular. Write the past simple form of these verbs in the correct column.

be	become	decide	have	like	live	make
meet	move	see	take	think	want	work

Regular	Irregular
liked	*was/were*
	became

10 Complete the sentences with some of the verbs from Exercise 9.

1 When I was twelve, my family _____ to Hong Kong.
2 At first, my brother and I _____ it was a wonderful place to live – so busy and lively.
3 We _____ in an apartment near the business district, and we _____ a lot of new people.
4 But our father and mother both _____ very hard in their new jobs and they were never at home.
5 We soon _____ bored with our life there and _____ to move back home.

11 Use the past simple to complete the article about an interesting living situation.

When did Brenda Kelly (1) _____ (become) interested in very small houses? When she was just thirteen years old. She (2) _____ (draw) plans and pictures and (3) _____ (dream) of building her own small house.

A few years later, she (4) _____ (be) ready for a house, but she (5) _____ (not have) a lot of money to spend on it. One day, she (6) _____ (see) some shipping containers at a container terminal* and she (7) _____ (think) it would be cool to live in one.

Brenda (8) _____ (not be) sure it was possible to make a house from a container. She did research and found people who (9) _____ (make) houses with materials that used to be something else. It (10) _____ (not take) long for her to find help and start building.

terminal *a dock or port where ships load and offload goods*

12 Work in pairs. Answer the questions.

1 Is Brenda's house made from new materials?
2 What did the house use to be?
3 What are some changes you think she made?

Check your answers on page 130. Do Exercises 4 and 5.

used to

My dad **used to** work in a bank.

We **didn't use to** live in a container house; we lived in an apartment.

Did you **use to** visit the city centre a lot? No, we **didn't**.

13 Look at the Grammar box. Answer the questions.

1 Do the sentences say exactly when the past habits, routines or states happened?
2 How do we form questions and negatives with *used to*?
3 Can we use the past simple to talk about past habits, routines or states as well as *used to*?

Check your answers on page 130. Do Exercises 4 and 5.

14 Choose the correct options to complete the text.

Brenda Kelly's house (1) *travels / used to travel* the world on trucks, trains and boats carrying products from place to place. But shipping containers (2) *aren't / didn't use to be* the only building material that (3) *are / used to be* something else.

In the mountains of Chile, there's a house that (4) *flies / used to fly* – because (5) *it's / it used to be* an old aeroplane. And at a farm in the Netherlands, you can stay in a train hotel that (6) *carries / used to carry* passengers every day – and it has a kitchen sink (7) *that's / that used to be* a car tyre!

15 PRONUNCIATION /zd/ and /st/ in *used*

a Look at the pronunciation box and listen to the examples. 🎧 9

When we say the past simple of *use*, we say /juːzd/, with a /z/ and /d/ sound:

*Some people in Chile **used** an old aeroplane as a house.*

When we use *used to* to describe a habit or situation in the past, we say /juːst/ with an /s/ and /t/ sound.

*Brenda Kelly's house **used to** travel the world.*

b Listen to the sentences and tick (√) the sound you hear. 🎧 9

	/juːzd/	/juːst/		/juːzd/	/juːst/
1	☐	☐	4	☐	☐
2	☐	☐	5	☐	☐
3	☐	☐	6	☐	☐

16 Have there been any changes in your house or neighbourhood? Describe them to a partner with *used to*. Use the correct pronunciation.

2B My space

All the comforts of home

An astronaut looks at Earth out of a porthole (a window) on the International Space Station.

VOCABULARY BUILDING Suffix *-ion*

> We can use the suffix *-ion* to make the noun form of many common verbs. There are several ways to do this:
>
> *-ion*: communicate → communication
>
> *-ation*: imagine → imagination
>
> Add *-ion* to the end of the word: direct → direction

1 Read the Vocabulary building box. Then complete the table. Use a dictionary if necessary. Listen and check your answers. 🎧 **10**

Verb	Noun
accommodate	(1) accommodation
construct	(2) construction
direct	(3) direction
educate	(4) education
(5) explore	exploration
locate	(6) location
(7) transport	transport / transportation

2 PRONUNCIATION Word stress

Listen again and underline the stressed syllable in each word. Which words have a different stress in the verb form and noun form? 🎧 **10**

3 Complete the text with words from Exercise 1.

The International Space Station is a base for space (1) _exploration_ and research. It travels 400 kilometres (249 miles) above the Earth, always moving in an east-to-west (2) _direction_ . Moving at 28,000 kilometres (17, 398 miles) per hour, it passes over the same (3) _location_ on Earth every four minutes. Rockets (4) _transport_ astronauts to and from the ISS, which can (5) _accommodate_ six astronauts at one time.

READING

4 Work in pairs. Look at the photo. Discuss the questions.

- What things in the photo do you have in your own bedroom?
- What do you think these rooms are like in a space station: bathroom, kitchen, living room, dining room?

said Japanese engineer Koichi Wakata as he was giving a video tour of his bedroom in the International Space Station (ISS). 'It's a little taller than my height. There's a sleeping bag here, which is very comfortable.
5 It's fixed* to the wall so I don't float away.' Wakata, who lived on the ISS three different times, had two computers in his room: one for official ISS business and a second for internet access. He also had a camera and earphones for communication with family and friends back home on Earth. His room also had a small lamp for reading in
10 bed, but instead of a wardrobe for his clothes, he kept them in a small storage locker. There simply wasn't room for a table or chair.

The ISS accommodation didn't offer Wakata many luxuries, but it provided a lot of the basic comforts of a usual home. He and the other astronauts ate packaged food in a small kitchen and dining
15 area, which had an oven but no fridge. Wakata couldn't have a shower in the ISS, but Italian astronaut Samantha Cristoforetti, who spent 199 days on the space station, explained that when she was living there, every astronaut had an area where they washed, brushed their teeth and so on. 'But you don't have a sink,' she explains. When
20 she was washing, she used very small amounts of water from small containers and a special 'no-rinse' soap and shampoo.

As astronaut Scott Kelly tweeted, 'All the comforts of home. Well, most of them.'

telephone box *a small booth where people could use public phones*
fixed *stuck, fastened*

The International Space Station (ISS) timeline

1984 The US government decided to build a space station for scientific research, education and space exploration.

1990s The Russian, Canadian, Japanese and European space programmes agreed to help with the construction.

1998 The Russian space agency sent the first part of the ISS into space, working with the other countries.

1998 to 2009 Astronauts added to the ISS to improve the accommodation on it.

---

5 Read about skimming. Then skim the article. Choose the best description of the article (a–d).

> To skim, read a text quickly without focusing on all of the words. Only look for main ideas. Read the title and the first sentence of each paragraph, and notice familiar and repeated words throughout the text.

a It explains how engineers designed the living areas of the International Space Station.
b It gives examples of problems that astronauts have living in the International Space Station.
c It gives a description of the living areas in the International Space Station.
d It talks about how people will build homes on Mars.

6 Read the article and timeline. Choose the correct option to complete each sentence.

1 Koichi Wakata's *bedroom* / *bed* is the size of an old telephone box.
2 The bed is on the *floor* / *wall*.
3 His bedroom *does* / *doesn't* have a chair.
4 There *isn't* / *is* a fridge in the kitchen area.
5 There isn't *water* / *a sink* for washing.
6 In 1984, the US government decided *to construct* / *construction* the ISS.
7 *Australia* / *Japan* helped build the ISS.
8 The first part went into space in *1998* / *2009*.

CRITICAL THINKING Analyze fact and opinion

> A fact is something that is true for everyone, for example, *Tokyo is in Japan*. An opinion is something you believe, but you can't prove, for example *Tokyo is the world's most exciting city*. We often mix fact and opinion when we communicate, so it's important to think about what is fact and what is opinion.

7 Look at the Critical thinking box. Are the sentences fact (F) or opinion (O)?

1 The bedroom is small. F
2 The sleeping bag is very comfortable. O
3 A computer provides internet access. F
4 Working in space, away from family, is very difficult. O
5 The food in space isn't very tasty. O
6 There's no shower on the ISS. F

8 Work in pairs. Follow these steps.

1 Scott Kelly thinks that the ISS has most of the comforts of home. Do you agree or disagree? Why?
2 a Make a list of eight things to take with you to live on the ISS. You will have basic food and water but you may choose to bring special food or drinks.
b Now remove four things from the list.
c What is the most important item on your list?

Rows of canal boats and houseboats

2C A unique style

GRAMMAR Past continuous

1 Can you remember who did what, according to the article? Match the two parts of the sentences.

1 When he was living on the ISS, Koichi Wakata
2 When Samantha Cristoforetti was working in space, she
3 When Scott Kelly was doing his research, he

a washed with 'no-rinse' soap.
b sometimes stopped to send tweets back to Earth.
c often spoke with friends and family at home.

Past continuous
*Koichi Wakata **was giving** a tour of his bedroom in the ISS.*
*Koichi Wakata **wasn't living** on the space station when he described his bedroom there.*
*When Samantha Cristoforetti **was living** there, every astronaut had an area where they washed.*

2 Look at the Grammar box. Choose the correct options to make rules about the past continuous.

1 The bold expressions describe *completed actions or events / general situations* in the past.
2 All of them are formed with the past simple of *be / have* and a verb in the *-ed / -ing* form.

3 Read the article. For each verb in bold, write S (ongoing past situation) or A (past action or event).

The perfect home

When Charlotte Tindle (1) **was preparing** to move to London to study music, her college (2) **suggested** student housing at a price of £1,000 per month. That's £36,000 for three years! The Tindles (3) **were making** plans to pay for Charlotte's housing when Mr Tindle (4) **had** an idea: why not spend the money on a houseboat and then sell it afterwards? And so the family (5) **bought** one. While they (6) **were cleaning** and (7) **repairing** the boat, friends (8) **joined** in and helped. Charlotte says that living in her unusual house is an adventure, but 'it is my home,' she says.

| 1 _S_ | 3 _S_ | 5 _A_ | 7 _S_ |
| 2 _A_ | 4 _A_ | 6 _S_ | 8 _A_ |

Check your answers on page 130. Do Exercises 6–8.

4 Read the article in Exercise 3 again. Disagree with these statements.

1 Charlotte wasn't expecting to leave home.
Yes, she was. She was preparing to move to London to study music.

2 Before she went to college, Charlotte was living with a roommate.
3 Charlotte was planning to live on a boat when she went to college.
4 The Tindles were expecting the college to pay for Charlotte's housing.
5 The Tindles were relaxing while Charlotte's friends cleaned the boat.

2. No she wasn't. She was living at home.

3. No she wasn't. She was planning to live in student housing.

4. No they weren't. They were expecting to pay for it themselves.

5. No they weren't. They were cleaning + repairing it.

5 Complete the text with the past simple or past continuous of the verbs in brackets.

Coming together and mixing

When Yinka Ilori (1) _was growing up_ (grow up), his parents often (2) _advised_ (advise) him to think about becoming an engineer. Instead, when he finished high school, he (3) _chose_ (choose) to study furniture design. Three years after he (4) _graduated_ (graduate), while he (5) _was trying_ (try) to develop his own style, he (6) _did_ (do) a project where he took two old chairs and made them into one new one. He then (7) _realised_ (realize) that his work was about storytelling and different cultures coming together and mixing. He (8) _was developing_ (develop) these ideas when an art expert (9) _found_ (find) his work online and invited him to show it at Milan Design Week – the world's largest design fair.

6 Use the words to make questions. Then ask and answer the questions with a partner.

1 parents / when / Ilori's / advise / to think / did / him / engineering / about / ?

When did Ilori's parents advise him to think about engineering?
- When he was growing up.

2 Ilori / study / what / choose / did / to / ?

3 two / Ilori / was doing / chairs / when / made / into / he / what / one / ?

4 did / when he / Ilori / what / realize / two / into / chairs / one / made / ?

5 found / Ilori's / when he / work / was developing his / who / online / ideas / ? *Who found it work when he was developing his online ideas?*

7 PRONUNCIATION *-ing* in fast speech

Read the Pronunciation box. Then listen and tick (√) the sentences you hear (a or b). 🔊 **12**

> Often, especially in fast speech, *-ing* in continuous verb forms is spoken as *-in*.

1 I didn't find what I wanted.
  a I was looking for the furniture shop.
  b I'll look in the furniture shop.

2 I saw you at the art competition.
  a Did you put in a painting?
  b Were you putting up paintings?

3 Are you hungry?
  a We were going to eat at four.
  b We go in to eat at four.

Yinka Ilori 'upcycles' old tables and chairs. He says, 'The UK is a very multicultural place: there are so many cultures here …, and it's nice to try and put that into furniture.'

8 CHOOSE

1 When Charlotte Tindle was looking for a home, she found an amazing way to live. Think of three important events in your life related to your home. In pairs, explain the ongoing situation and the single action or event.

My family was living in Athens when my little brother was born.

2 When Yinka Ilori was working on an art project, he discovered his interest in different cultures coming together. Think about something you love doing or are very interested in. Write about what was happening in your life when you discovered it. Explain how you have learned more about it.

I was watching a music video when a thought hit me: I want to learn the guitar. I didn't have a hobby at the time, so I asked my parents for guitar lessons.

3 Instead of writing about your hobby or other interest, prepare a presentation about it.

AUTHENTIC LISTENING SKILLS

Listening for gist

When you listen, don't try to understand every word. Try to relax and focus on what you do understand, not what you don't understand. Notice words that the speaker repeats or stresses, and the types of words that are used a lot, for example, adjectives. Try to work out the connections between the words you understand.

1 Listen to to the extract from the TED Talk. Circle the topics Elora talks about. 🎧 **13**

a doors
b windows
c shapes
d construction materials

2 What is the general idea of what she is talking about? Write a sentence.

3 Share your idea with a partner.

WATCH

4 Look at the photo on page 20 and read the caption. Why do you think it might it be important to use local materials, like bamboo in Bali, to build houses?

5 Watch Part 1 of the talk. Choose the correct option to complete each sentence. ▶ **2.1**

1 _____ drew a fairy mushroom house.
 a When Elora was a child, her mother
 b Last year, Elora
 c When she was a child, Elora

2 The curved roof helps keep the house _____.
 a dry   **b** cool   **c** warm

3 It's easy to _____ a person who is using the bathroom.
 a hear   **b** see   **c** avoid

6 Watch Part 2 of the talk. Are the sentences true (T) or false (F)? ▶ **2.2**

1 Bamboo is a grass.
2 Bamboo grows very slowly.
3 Bamboo is light and strong.
4 Hardy plans to build a school from bamboo.
5 The Green School used sustainable materials.

7 Watch Part 3 of the talk. Choose the correct option to complete each sentence. ▶ **2.3**

1 Elora says it is important to *make bamboo do what you want / design for bamboo's strengths*.
2 Elora builds models of her houses to *help sell houses to her customers / to test the design*.
3 She prefers to build doors that are *balanced / not shaped like teardrops*.
4 Bamboo grows back quickly, so it is *a safe / an environmentally friendly* material.

8 VOCABULARY IN CONTEXT

a Watch the clips from the TED Talk. Choose the correct meanings of the words. ▶ 2.4

b Answer the questions.

1 What is one thing that just *doesn't feel right* in your town or city?
2 Has someone ever *just had to tell you* something? What was it?
3 Who is one person who has *treated you well*?
4 In your city, what material *makes perfect sense* to build with?
5 Think of someone you know who is *elegant*. Why would you describe them like this?

9 Work in pairs. Read the extract from the talk. Discuss the questions.

The floor that you walk on, can it affect the way that you walk? Can it change the footprint that you'll ultimately leave on the world?

1 Is Elora talking about an actual floor?
2 How can the floor we walk on change our *footprint*?
3 We can't all build bamboo houses. What else can we do in our homes to change the footprint we leave?
4 What kind of footprint will you leave on the world? Why?

10 MY PERSPECTIVE

Work in small groups. Discuss the questions.

- As a child, Elora's dream house looked like a mushroom. What is your idea of a dream house?
- Elora designs her houses to be comfortable in hot weather. What is the weather like where you live? How do you make your house comfortable?
- How are Elora's houses similar to your house? How are they different?
- Would you like to live in one of Elora's houses? Why? / Why not? What are the good and bad things about them, in your opinion?

CHALLENGE

Think of the dream house you described in Exercise 10. Do the following:

- Decide what material you would build with: wood, brick, bamboo, something else?
- Decide how it will work with the environment. How will it stay comfortable in hot or cold weather?
- Draw a plan for the house and label the rooms and other details in the house. Include as many rooms as you like – a music room, a cinema, etc.

2E Special things, special places

SPEAKING

1 Work in pairs. Discuss the questions.

- For you, is the idea of living alone on a tropical island an exciting or scary idea?
- Think back to your answers to Exercise 8 on page 25 about what you would like to take with you to live on the ISS. Would your answers be different for life on a tropical island? For example, what clothes would you take? How would you protect yourself from the sun? How would you get food?
- What parts of civilization would you miss the most?

2 Listen to the conversation. Are the sentences true (T) or false (F)? 🎧 14

1 David became rich and, as a result, he bought the island.
2 There was a small community of people already living on the island, so David joined them.
3 Denika left because she wasn't completely comfortable on the island.
4 The reason David has electricity on the island is that he set up a solar power system.
5 David says that moving to the island was a big mistake because he's not happy living alone.

3 Read the Useful language box. Then, in small groups, take turns giving the reasons for the items you talked about taking to a tropical island in Exercise 1. Try to use all of the expressions in the box.

I'd want a computer because …
I'd need a mobile phone, so …
The reason I'd want a music system is …
I'd need a swimsuit as …

4 Think of five things that you use every day. Explain why they are important to you, using the Useful language.

I need my backpack every day because …

5 Do you think your items would still be useful on a tropical island? With a group of three, plan a list of ten items to take. Give reasons for each item.

Useful language

Giving reasons

Use *The reason …, because, so* and *as* to give reasons.

The reason he went there was to get away from his money problems.

He went because his business failed.

She thought life was too hard, so she left.

As he loved living a simple life in a tiny house, he didn't want to leave.

**Shuri Castle in
Naha, Japan**

WRITING A description

6 Think of a home that you really like (but not your own home). It can be a place you have seen or visited – a friend's house, a family home or a famous place such as a castle. Answer the questions.

1 Where is it?
2 When did you go there?
3 How old is it?
4 Why is it special? The location? The way it looks?
5 Who lives there (or used to live there)?
6 What did you see or do there?

7 Read the description on page 149. Answer the questions.

1 Where is Shuri castle?
2 When did Kana go there?
3 How old is it?
4 Why is it special?
5 Who used to live there?
6 What did Kana do there?

8 Write six general questions that you can use to write about any visit to a place. Use the words in the Writing strategies box.
Who lives there? / Who used to live there?

9 **WRITING SKILL** Using adjectives

a Look at the description on page 149. Underline the adjectives the writer uses to describe the castle.

b We use adjectives to make descriptions more interesting. Which adjectives can you use to describe the home you chose in Exercise 6?

10 Write a short description of the home you talked about in Exercise 6.

11 Exchange descriptions with a partner. Check each other's work.
Does your partner's description answer all of the questions from Exercise 6?
Does it use adjectives?

> ### Writing strategies
>
> **Describing a visit to a place**
>
> You can describe a visit to a place by answering the questions *Who?, What?, When?, Where?, Why?* and *How?*

3 Health and happiness

This teen in Tokyo, Japan, shows that good food can make people both healthy and happy.

3A Treating the whole person

VOCABULARY Being well

1 Work in pairs. Look at the photo and discuss the questions. What is the boy happy about? What things do people need to be happy?

2 Tick (√) the parts of the body that you can see in the photo.

arm	shoulder	chest	ear
elbow	finger	foot	hand
head	knee	leg	mouth
neck	nose	stomach	throat

3 Look at the photo. What parts of the body can tell you if a person is happy?

4 Read the article. Match the words in bold (1–11) with the definitions (a–k).

A doctor in the jungle

In Cameroon, it isn't always easy to find a (1) **hospital** when you're (2) **unwell**. But if you're lucky, a doctor may find you. Almost every weekend, Dr Georges Bwelle and his assistants take care of the (3) **health** needs of about 500 people in small villages in the jungle. They see (4) **patients** with a variety of (5) **illnesses** and (6) **injuries** and give people (7) **medicine**. Dr Bwelle also provides items that people need to make their lives better, like (8) **glasses**. Why does he do it? Helping people to be (9) **healthy** brings a lot of (10) **happiness** to Dr Bwelle. 'To make people laugh, to reduce the (11) **pain**, that's why I'm doing this,' he says.

a problems with the body or the mind
b the condition of someone's body and mind
c a bad feeling
d something worn over the eyes to help you see
e something to make you feel better when you are ill
f people who are ill and need help from a doctor
g the condition of feeling good and not sad
h a place where ill and injured people get treatment
i ill
j well, not ill
k when a part of the body is hurt

5 Are these words illnesses (IL), injuries (IN), or symptoms* (S)? Use a dictionary if necessary. Check your answers with a partner.

a broken arm	a virus
the flu	pain
a headache	seasickness
a stomachache	a high temperature
a broken leg	a backache

symptom *a change in the body that shows you are ill or injured*

6 MY PERSPECTIVE

Work in pairs. Discuss the questions.

- Do you do anything to stay healthy? Eat certain foods? Exercise? Something else?
- When you're ill or hurt, do you take medicine? Why? / Why not? If so, what kind? Do you try anything else to deal with the problem?

LISTENING

7 Complete the questionnaire about your experience of going to the doctor. You can tick (√) more than one answer for each question.

1 When or why do you go to the doctor?

☐ because of an illness
☐ for a check-up (a routine health check)
☐ to talk about a problem you have
☐ for school
☐ other reasons

2 What does the doctor usually do?

☐ check my height and weight
☐ check my eyes and ears
☐ give me medicine
☐ ask questions about my health and happiness (*Have you been sick? Do you feel any pain?*)
☐ ask about symptoms

3 What other things does the doctor talk to you about?

☐ family
☐ food
☐ staying healthy (exercise, getting enough sleep, etc.)
☐ sleep
☐ school
☐ staying safe (wearing a seatbelt, not smoking, using sunscreen)
☐ other things

8 Work in pairs. Compare your answers to Exercise 7 and discuss the questions.

- Do you both go to the doctor for the same reasons?
- Is the doctor the only person you see when you go? Who else might you see?
- Do you talk to the doctor about other things in your life? Why? / Why not?

9 Read the sentences. Then listen to a lecture about 'whole-person' health care. Tick (√) the ideas that the speaker discusses. 🎧 **15**

1 Today, finding new medicines is the world's biggest problem.
2 Many doctors look after a person's health and happiness, not only a patient's illness.
3 Sometimes people think they are ill, but really, the problem is just in their mind.
4 The World Health Organization says that many hospitals need to think more about people and the world they live in.
5 Dr Paul Tournier believed that only medicine could make people healthy.

10 Work in pairs. Listen to the lecture again. Answer the questions. 🎧 **15**

1 What examples of common health problems does the speaker give?
2 What did Dr Tournier mean by 'the whole person?'
3 What does the World Health Organization say that health is connected to?
4 What do 'whole-person' doctors talk about with their patients?
5 What can help us stay healthy, according to the lecture?

11 MY PERSPECTIVE

Work in small groups. Discuss the questions.

- Do you visit the same doctor for all health problems, or do you visit different doctors?
- Is your doctor an 'illness' doctor or a 'whole-person' doctor? Which type of doctor do you prefer? Why?
- Is there anything you would like your doctor to do differently? What?

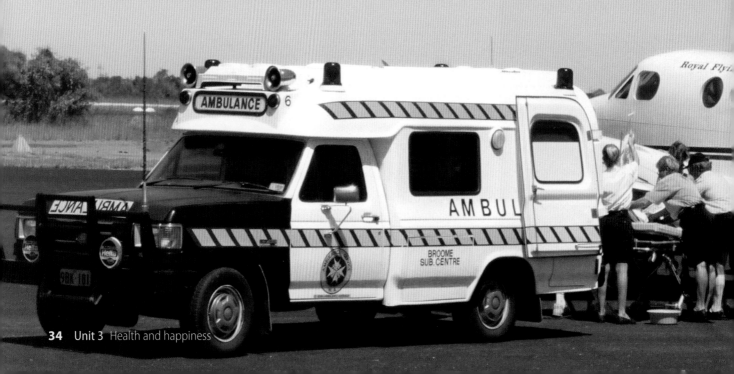

GRAMMAR Quantifiers, *how much / many*?

12 Look at the sentences in the Grammar box. Underline the words that express or ask about quantity.

Quantifiers

a ... *some doctors and nurses still think about illnesses.*

b ... *many doctors and nurses still need to change.*

c *Doctors might ask a few questions about food ...*

d *Do you eat a lot of fruit and vegetables?*

e *That's why the doctor tells you ... to eat only a little sugar.*

f *How much stress do you have in your life?*

13 Look at the words and expressions you have underlined in Exercise 11. Answer the questions.

1 Which words go with countable nouns? Which ones go with uncountable nouns?
2 In sentences a–e, which words describe a large number or amount? Which ones describe a small number or amount?
3 Which other words do you know that express quantity?

Check your answers on page 132. Do Exercises 1–5.

14 Choose the correct options to complete the text.

Nature's pharmacy
(1) *A lot of / Many of* the medicine we use today comes from plants. For example, aspirin, a common pain medicine, used to come from (2) *some / a* tree. An important cancer drug comes from Pacific yew trees, but after (3) *some / any* years of cutting them down, there weren't (4) *some / many* trees left. Then in the 1990s, scientists learned how to make the medicine without killing the trees, or even causing (5) *many / much* damage. A (6) *few / little* health products also come from animals. For example, (7) *many / much* people take (8) *a few / a little* fish oil in their diet to stay healthy.

15 Complete the questions with *How much* or *How many*. Listen to the interview and check your answers. 🎧 16

1 _____ plants in Tanzania can you use as medicine?
2 _____ traditional doctors did you interview?
3 _____ time did you spend on the project?
4 _____ information did you collect?

16 Listen again. Write the answers to Amy's questions. 🎧 16

17 Work in pairs. Think of three *How much* and three *How many* questions to ask each other about health, diet, exercise, etc.

18 PRONUNCIATION Contrastive stress

Look at the Pronunciation box. Then listen and match each sentence with the correct meaning (a–d). 🎧 17

> We use contrastive stress to show meaning. Listen to the stress in these sentences.
> How **many** different plants are there in Tanzania?
> (I want to know the number.)
> How many different **plants** are there in Tanzania?
> (I'm interested in plants, not animals.)
> How many different plants are there in **Tanzania**?
> (I'm interested in Tanzania, not Kenya.)

I drink a little milk every day.

1 _____ 2 _____ 3 _____ 4 _____

a I never miss a day. c I don't drink a little soda.
b I don't drink a lot. d My brother doesn't drink any.

Services like the Royal Flying Doctor Service in Australia work to provide medical care for people in remote areas.

VH-KFN

3B Painless

VOCABULARY BUILDING Synonyms

A synonym is a word that has a similar meaning to another word. Writers often use synonyms to add variety to a text. Synonyms should be the same part of speech. One way to check if two words are synonyms is to use the words in the same place in a sentence. If the sentences have the same meaning, the words are synonyms.

1 For each pair, read the first sentence from an article about a girl who doesn't feel pain. Then complete the second sentence with a synonym of the word in bold.

block	calm	frightening	realize	sore

1 Ashlyn Blocker was a **quiet** baby.
Her parents felt lucky to have such a _____ child.

2 It was red and looked **painful**.
The doctor carefully touched her _____ eye.

3 At first, he didn't **understand**.
After checking, he began to _____ that Ashlyn wasn't like most other kids.

4 'It was **scary**,' says her mother.
That idea was very _____ .

5 Now doctors are studying Ashlyn to understand how her body can **stop** pain.
It may help them to develop new medicines to _____ pain.

READING

2 Read about understanding the time and order of events. Then read the article. Number the events from the article in the correct order.

Understanding the time and order of events can help you understand the whole text. Look for dates, ages, time expressions such as *When . . .* and adverbs of order such as *then*, *after that* and *next*.

a Ashlyn has something wrong with her eye.
b Ashlyn's doctors discover other people with the same illness.
c The doctor discovers that Ashlyn doesn't feel pain.
d Doctors study Ashlyn to learn more.
e Ashlyn's parents feel lucky. *1*
f Ashlyn's parents feel unlucky.
g Her parents take her to the doctor.

3 Read the article again. Choose the correct option to complete each sentence.

1 As a baby, Ashlyn Blocker didn't cry because
   a she was never hungry.   b she didn't feel pain.
   c she was a quiet child.

2 Her parents took her to the doctor because she
   a didn't cry.   b was upset.
   c had an eye problem.

3 Feeling no pain is dangerous because you can easily
   a injure yourself.   b hurt someone else.
   c become ill.

4 Ashlyn's illness is
   a common in some places.   b very unusual.
   c often seen in young babies.

5 Doctors may use Ashlyn's case to help people who
   a can't feel or smell anything.   b have a lot of pain.
   c have eye problems.

6 For Ashlyn, feeling no pain is
   a very strange.   b normal.
   c something she loves.

4 Work in pairs. Discuss the questions.

   • When might Ashlyn's condition be good or helpful?
   • What skills or habits do you think Ashlyn developed to deal with her condition?
   • What does the photo tell you about Ashlyn?

CRITICAL THINKING Making ideas clear

To make sure their ideas are clear, writers often:
• report what someone said.
• give examples.
• say the same thing using different words.

5 Read the Critical thinking box. Then find the ideas below in the article. Which strategy does the writer use to make each idea clear?

1 As a small baby, Ashlyn Blocker seemed very happy.
2 Pain is necessary.
3 Pain keeps us from danger.
4 Mr and Mrs Blocker were afraid for their daughter.
5 Ashlyn isn't the only person with her condition.
6 Ashlyn is comfortable with her condition.

6 Work in pairs. Discuss the questions.

   • Which ideas in the text would you like to know more about?
   • What questions would you like to ask Ashlyn, her parents or her doctors?

Feeling
NO PAIN

🎧 **18** Ashlyn Blocker was a quiet baby. She didn't cry even when she was hungry. At first, her parents felt lucky to have such a calm child. But then, when Ashlyn was eight months old, Mr and Mrs Blocker noticed a problem
5 with her eye. It was red and looked painful, so they took her to the doctor. As he checked Ashlyn, the doctor carefully touched her sore eye. Patients – especially babies and children – usually don't like this and they try to move away. Ashlyn didn't do this. The doctor was surprised
10 and, at first, he didn't understand. But after checking, he began to realize that Ashlyn wasn't like most other kids because Ashlyn didn't feel pain. Her body turned pain off.

You may think this sounds like a good thing – no pain means never getting hurt, right? But we feel pain for a
15 reason. It has an important purpose: it tells us that our body has an injury or illness. Pain also helps to keep us safe. When a child touches a hot oven, the pain says 'Danger!' and stops a more serious injury.

After discovering that their daughter couldn't feel pain,
20 the Blockers no longer felt lucky. 'It was scary,' says her mother, Tara Blocker, because Ashlyn could easily injure herself and not know it. That idea was very frightening. As Ashlyn began to grow up and started to move around more, and to walk, keeping her safe every day became
25 more and more of a challenge.

No one had ever come to Ashlyn's doctors with this condition*, and at first they thought she might be the only case in the world. But they found out that there were others with the condition – a whole family in
30 Pakistan and eight other kids who lived nearer to Ashlyn, in the US.

Now doctors are studying Ashlyn and other people who don't feel pain. They want to understand the condition and help people
35 who have it. But they also want to understand how the body can stop pain. It may help them to develop new medicines to block pain – good news for anyone who experiences a lot of it.

What's it like to feel no pain? Ashlyn deals with the condition well and has a happy life. She says, 'It's just me. It's all I've ever known.'

condition *health problem*

'It's just me. It's all I've ever known.'

Ashlyn Blocker

3C What makes us happy?

GRAMMAR Phrasal verbs

1 Look at the sentences in the Grammar box. Underline the verbs.

> **Phrasal verbs**
>
> *Ashlyn's body turned pain **off**.*
>
> *As Ashlyn began to grow **up** and started to move around more …*
>
> *They found **out** that there were others with the condition.*
>
> *Ashlyn deals **with** the condition well and has a happy life.*

2 Answer the questions about the sentences in the Grammar box.

 1 What part of speech are the words in bold?
 2 These words combine with verbs to make phrasal verbs. Do they come before or after the verb?
 3 What's different about the first one?

Check your answers on page 132. Do Exercises 6–10.

3 Are these phrasal verbs separable or inseparable? Try putting them into sentences. Write S or I. Then check your answers on page 132.

1	put on	**6**	hand in
2	turn on	**7**	look into
3	get on (with)	**8**	look after
4	give up	**9**	work out (at the gym)
5	hang out	**10**	take out

WHAT MAKES TEENS HAPPY?

 • Good health
 • Exercise
 • Good diet (a lot of fresh fruit, eating breakfast)
 • Enjoying school
 • Friendly classmates

Source: World Health Organization

4 Read the information about research carried out by the World Health Organization. Match each statement below with a reason for happiness.

 1 My school friends and I **get on** well – they're nice.
 2 I go to the gym and **work out** once or twice a week.
 3 I **gave up** sugary foods. I also have a bowl of cereal every morning.
 4 I almost always **hand in** my homework on time. I don't mind doing it.
 5 I'm not ill very often because I **look after** myself.

5 Find the two sentences in Exercise 4 with phrasal verbs that can have the particle after the object. Rewrite them with the phrasal verbs separated.

6 Complete the sentences using phrasal verbs from Exercises 1–3. Then listen to the conversation and check your answers. 🎧 19

1 Some scientists _____ teenagers' happiness.

2 Did they _____ what makes us happy?

3 I feel happy when I _____ my headphones _____ and listen to some music.

4 For me, it's TV. I always feel happy when I _____ it _____ .

5 Happy teenagers _____ with their friends a lot.

6 I _____ the rubbish _____ every day!

7 Listen to the conversation again. What things do the speakers say make teenagers unhappy? 🎧 19

8 Look at the facts about what makes teens unhappy. Then complete the advice with verbs and particles from the chart below. Two particles are used twice.

WHAT MAKES TEENS UNHAPPY?

- Poor health
- No exercise, a lot of TV
- Poor diet (a lot of sugary foods, no breakfast)
- School stress/not having time to do schoolwork
- Bullying

Verbs

deal	give	hand	look	put	take	turn

Particles

after	in	off	up	with

Advice

1 _____ yourself so you don't become ill.

2 _____ a sport or another physical activity.

3 _____ drinking sweet drinks, like cola, every day. Save them as a weekend treat.

4 Don't _____ your homework _____ . _____ it _____ on time.

5 _____ bullying by telling an adult about it. Ask for help.

6 Don't watch TV just because it's on. You can always _____ it _____ !

9 MY PERSPECTIVE

What do *you* think helps make people happy? Use these verbs or your own ideas. Write five sentences. Then discuss your sentences with a partner.

belonging to …	dealing with …
giving up …	looking after …
putting on …	talking to friends about …
taking up …	

I think belonging to groups of similar people makes us happy.

10 CHOOSE

1 Work in a group. Discuss your sentences from Exercise 9 and decide which four sentences are best.

2 Use your sentences from Exercise 9 to make a poster called *What makes people happy?* Find photos or draw simple pictures to add to each point.

3 Write a short paragraph based on the information in Exercise 4. Give an example for each point. Use phrasal verbs.

A boy jumps from the U Bein Bridge into Taungthaman Lake, Myanmar.

The amazing story of the man who gave us modern pain relief

" Bonica saw pain close up. He felt it. He lived it. And it made it impossible for him to ignore in others. "

LATIF NASSER

Read about Latif Nasser and get ready to watch his TED Talk. ▶ **3.0**

AUTHENTIC LISTENING SKILLS

Collaborative listening

When you listen to authentic speech, you usually won't understand everything you hear and you often can't go back and listen again. However, different people often understand different parts of a message. You can increase your understanding by comparing listening notes with others.

1 Read the Authentic listening skills box. Then listen to the extract from the TED Talk and write down the words you remember. 🎧 **20**

2 Work in small groups. Compare notes on what you heard. Did you write the same words? Write a summary of what you heard as a group. Do you have more information now?

3 Listen to the extract again. Did you understand more this time? Tell a partner what the extract means. 🎧 **20**

WATCH

4 Think of a time when you saw or experienced an event that changed the way you thought about something. What happened? How did it change you? Make some notes. Compare your ideas with a partner.

5 Watch Part 1 of the talk. Choose the correct option to complete each sentence. ▶ **3.1**

1 The lion tamer's main problem was that
  a the lion bit him.
  b he couldn't breathe with his head in the lion's mouth.
  c he was scared.

2 The strongman gave the lion tamer _____ to save his life.
  a mouth to mouth
  b medicine
  c an operation

3 The strongman worked at the circus to help pay for
  a a new car.
  b healthcare.
  c medical school.

4 At the army hospital, Bonica's job was
  a helping patients with pain.
  b doing amputations.
  c looking after the whole hospital.

5 Pain is a signal for
  a fear.
  b an injury.
  c being tired.

6 He was surprised that many patients felt _____ when the injury was better.
  a very angry
  b a lot of pain
  c ready to go home

6 Watch Part 2 of the talk. Choose the correct option to complete each sentence. ▶ 3.2

1 Bonica often discussed pain with *other doctors / patients' families*.

2 Bonica read medical books and found that they gave *a lot of / only a little* information about pain.

3 To get more people talking about pain, Bonica *tried to get experts to write about it / wrote about it himself*.

4 Bonica didn't want to just make his patients healthier, he wanted to *be famous / make them feel better*.

5 Now there are *only a few / hundreds of* pain clinics around the world.

6 Bonica understood pain well because he *felt a lot of / read a lot about* pain.

7 Think about Parts 1 and 2 of the talk. What evidence does Latif give to support these statements?

1 Bonica 'inflicted (caused) pain, and he treated it.'

2 'Bonica saw pain close up. He felt it. He lived it.'

3 Bonica's 'goal wasn't to make patients better; it was to make patients feel better.'

8 VOCABULARY IN CONTEXT

a Watch the clips from the talk. Choose the correct meaning of the words and phrases. ▶ 3.3

b Work in pairs. Answer the questions. Then compare your answers with your partner.

1 Have you ever had a problem and tried to *ignore* it? What happened?

2 When do you usually *hit the books*? Where do you do it?

3 Have you ever *passed out*? Or has a friend or family member ever *passed out*? What happened?

4 Is there anyone in your family who is a *specialist* in a subject? Who? Which subject?

5 How many *institutions* can you name in your town/area? What kind of *institutions* are they?

6 When was the last time you felt that someone *didn't take you seriously*? Who was it? How did you feel?

CHALLENGE

Bonica did a lot of good in the world, making life better for people in pain. Think of a teacher, doctor, nurse, scientist, politician, sportsperson or someone else you know about who has helped people feel better. Make some notes about what they did.

Cristiano Ronaldo

– footballer

– gave money to a ten-year-old fan who needed medical help

– paid for a cancer centre in Portugal

9 Write a paragraph describing the person you made notes about in the Challenge box. Then compare your ideas with your partner. What things are similar about the people? What things are different?

3E Opinions about health and happiness

SPEAKING

1 Do you agree or disagree with the statements? Why? / Why not? Tell a partner.

- People should be free to smoke cigarettes anywhere.
- People should not be allowed to smoke in restaurants, cafes, cinemas and other public places.
- The government should ban (completely stop) smoking because it is bad for everyone's health and wellbeing.

2 Listen to the conversation. Who makes or agrees with each statement – Al (A), Marta (M), or both (B)? 🎧 21

1 Smoking should be completely forbidden.
2 Smoking should be allowed.
3 Smoking is bad for smokers' health.
4 Smoking is bad for everyone.
5 Everyone does something dangerous every day.
6 There's no real reason for anyone to smoke.

3 Work in small groups. For each topic, think of three or more arguments *for* the statement and three or more arguments *against* the statement.

- The government should ban junk food.
- Schools should make students get more exercise.
- Using a phone while walking or cycling should be illegal.
- Students shouldn't have to do a lot of homework.
- It's more important to have one very good friend than lots of friends.

4 Look at the phrases in the Useful language box. Working with another small group, take turns arguing for and against the points in Exercise 3.

Useful language

Giving your opinion
I think … / I believe …
In my opinion …

Disagreeing
Really / Are you kidding? I'm not sure about that.
I don't agree.
Sorry, but I don't think so.

Asking follow-up questions
Why do you say that?
Could you explain that a bit more?

Conceding a point
You're right that …
Well, that's true …

WRITING An opinion essay

5 Rank the ways to stay healthy in order from 1 (the most important) to 8 (the least important). Discuss your answers with a partner.

exercise every day
don't smoke cigarettes
see a doctor every six months
see friends and family

finish schoolwork on time
have a healthy diet
get plenty of sleep
wear a seatbelt

People ride their bikes through Bonsecours Basin Park in Montreal, Canada.

6 Read the essay on page 149. Answer the questions.

1 Does the writer agree or disagree with the statement 'Exercising every day is the best way to stay healthy'?
2 According to the writer, what does exercise sometimes make people do?
3 In addition to good food and exercise, what does the writer advise?

7 Read the Useful language box. Then read the essay again. Find five expressions from the box in the essay.

8 Read these expressions. In which category in the box does each belong?

I think this because …   *My view is that …*   *I accept that … , but …*

9 Work in pairs. Say if you agree or disagree with each statement and why.

1 Happiness is more important than health.
2 The best way to stay healthy is to stay happy.
3 It's more important to *feel* OK than to be healthy.

10 **WRITING SKILL** Organizing points in an essay

a Read the essay on page 149 again. How many main points does the writer make? How are these organized?
b How does the writer introduce each point? Which expressions does he / she use?
c Choose one of the statements you discussed in Exercise 9. Think of three points you can make about it and write a sentence introducing each one.

11 Write an essay about the statement you chose in Exercise 10c, saying whether you agree or disagree with it. Use the Useful language and your ideas from Exercise 10.

12 Exchange essays with a partner. Check each other's work and comment on the content. Does it use the Useful language correctly? Do you agree with your partner?

Useful language

Acknowledging other ideas
While it's true that … , I think …
Yes, you're right, but …

Giving your opinion
I believe …
In my opinion, …
For me, …

Giving reasons for your opinion
One reason I think this is …
I think it's clear that …
… because …

4 Learning

Students stand on their desks during a classroom activity in Maryland in the United States.

4A How we learn

VOCABULARY Education

① Work in pairs. Look at the photo. Find these items.

a blackboard	a desk	a notebook	a pen	a student	a teacher

② Match the verbs (1-6) with their objects (a-f). Use a dictionary if necessary.

1 develop	**a** geography / maths / science / art
2 study	**b** (good / bad) grades / an education
3 get	**c** (primary / secondary / private / state) school
4 take	**d** (new) skills
5 attend	**e** creative / hard-working
6 be	**f** a test / exams

③ Choose the correct options to complete the descriptions of three different schools.

- The Indian government provides (1) *state / private* schools for all children. But when students don't live near a school and can't afford to travel, it's difficult for them to get (2) *bad grades / an education*. The solution? Teachers travel to the students! (3) *Primary / Secondary* school students (up to age 12), and students in the first two years of (4) *primary / secondary* school (ages 13 and 14) can attend 'train platform schools'. The students are very (5) *creative / hard-working*. Some older students are even already at the station because they have jobs there!

- Students of the Khan Academy (6) *attend / study* geography, maths, science and other subjects online by watching videos. After watching, they can take short (7) *grades / tests* to check their progress. Most Khan Academy students are teens taking classes in addition to their usual studies. They want extra work to develop (8) *skills / studies* in certain subjects and to do better in exams. As the videos are online, students from around the world can (9) *take / get* the classes.

- Students who (10) *attend / get* the Zip Zap Circus School in Cape Town, South Africa, don't study maths and science; they (11) *take / learn* entertainment skills. Zip Zap is a private (12) *education / school*, but it isn't expensive. In fact, unlike most private schools, it's free. The main purpose of the school is to help students learn to live and work together – and to have fun.

④ Answer the questions. Take notes. Then compare your answers with a partner.

Which school ...

1 doesn't teach traditional school subjects? What does it teach?
2 is the most like your school? Why?
3 helps students trying to get very good grades or prepare for exams? How?

⑤ MY PERSPECTIVE

Work in pairs. Discuss the questions.

- Is your school a state school or a private school? What are the differences between the two? Think about cost, class size, teachers, building(s), etc.

- Which subjects from this list are you taking? Which classes are your favourites? Why?

arts (music, drama)	computing	history	language
literature	maths (algebra, geometry)	science (biology, chemistry)	

- Do any of your classes include online learning? Which one(s)?

LISTENING

6 Have you ever talked to a student from another country? If you have, what was it like? If not, would you like to? What are the benefits of talking to people from other countries?

7 Listen to two students talking about a project at school. Are the sentences true (T) or false (F)? 🎧 **22**

1 Karina's class is video-chatting with students around the world.
2 They are watching films to learn about each other's countries.
3 They learned about the school week in Japan.
4 They discussed school clothes in England.
5 Maria, in Brazil, is going to take an important examination soon.
6 Karina says that teenagers in other countries are very different.

8 Listen again. Complete the notes. 🎧 **22**

Karina's favourite class: (1) _____
Project: video-chatting with students in Brazil,
(2) _____ , Japan, England and
(3) _____
People usually learn about America from
(4) _____ .
Some Japanese kids go to school on Saturday for sports or to (5) _____ .
Kids in the UK start school at the age of (6) _____ .
Maria is taking extra classes in (7) _____ and
(8) _____ .
Teenagers everywhere have a lot in (9) _____ .

9 MY PERSPECTIVE

Work in pairs. Discuss the questions.

- Do you like the idea of video-chatting with students in other countries? Why? / Why not?
- Say two or three things you know about another country – about food, sports, weather, products they make, and so on. Where did you learn the information?
- What questions would you ask a student from another country? Think of one question about school and one question about another topic.

GRAMMAR Comparatives and superlatives

10 Look at the examples in the Grammar box. Answer the questions.

Comparative and superlative adjectives

Comparative
*Learning from a person is **more interesting than** learning from a book.*
*She's a bit **older than** we are.*
*Talking to someone is **easier than** reading.*

Superlative
*I think doing projects is **the best** way to learn.*

1 Which form uses *than* after an adjective?
2 Which form uses *the* before an adjective?
3 Which form compares more than two things?
4 Write the plain adjective forms for these items.
   more interesting   easier   older   the best

Check your answers on page 134. Do Exercises 1 and 2.

New communication technologies, like video-chatting, are helping students around the world connect and learn about each other.

11 Complete the sentences with the correct form of the adjectives.

1 Studying for a short time every day is _____ (useful) than studying all night the night before a test.
2 Breakfast is the _____ (important) meal.
3 A light lunch is _____ (good) than a big one because a big lunch can make you sleepy.
4 Studying is important, but the _____ (good) way to learn a new skill is by using it.
5 Learning a new language is _____ (easy) than learning maths or science.
6 It is _____ (difficult) to learn new things in the afternoon than in the morning.

12 Work in pairs. Discuss the sentences in Exercise 11. Do you agree with them?

13 Look at the examples in the Grammar box. Then answer the questions.

Comparative and superlative adverbs

a *I learn **better** by talking to people than by reading.*

b *Everyone works **the hardest** before important exams.*

1 Which sentence is comparative? Which is superlative?
2 What is the superlative adverb form of *good*?
3 What is the comparative adverb form of *hard*?
4 Do these sentences compare people/things or actions?

Check your answers on page 134. Do Exercises 3 and 4.

14 Complete the sentences with the comparative or superlative adverb forms of these words.

careful	good	hard	often	quiet	recent

1 I work _____ in history than I do in English.
2 Yusuf speaks _____ of all of us in class, so it's hard to hear him.
3 Ella graduated from high school _____ than Jim. She just finished last year.
4 My grades are improving. I did _____ in my final exam than in the mid-term one.
5 Pietro misses lessons _____ than the other students, because he isn't very well.
6 I checked the essay section of the test _____ because that's where I usually make a lot of mistakes.

15 Work in pairs. Discuss the questions.

- Which subject do you usually do best in?
- Do you find that you can learn more easily at some times than others? When? Why?
- Who studies the hardest in your class?

Students in a UN school talk to other students around the world.

16 **PRONUNCIATION** Linking and elision

Which two words in the example are connected by linking? Which two are connected by elision? 🎧 **23**

> Fluent speakers often join words together either by linking sounds (liaison) or leaving out sounds (elision).
>
> *I work harder in history than I do in English because it's more difficult to remember dates than words.*

17 Say the sentences. Do the bold words connect with linking or elision? Listen to check your answers. 🎧 **24**

1 Yusuf speaks the **most quietly**.
2 Ella graduated from school **more recently** than Jim.
3 I did **better in** my final exam than in the mid-term one.
4 Pietro misses lessons **more often** than the other students.
5 I **checked the** essay section the **most carefully**.

18 Make true sentences about you. Use comparatives and superlatives of the words in brackets. Then, share your ideas with a partner.

Compare ...

1 two school subjects. (difficult)
2 one school subject to the others. (easy)
3 the way two friends speak. (quiet)
4 how you work at two things. (hard)
5 forms of transport in your town/country. (comfortable)
6 forms of transport in your country. (cheap)

I think maths is more difficult than English. For me, art is the easiest subject.

Nothing's impossible

VOCABULARY BUILDING Suffixes -ful/-less

We can create adjectives by adding a suffix to some nouns. The suffix -ful means with and -less means without. But be careful – you can't always make opposites using -ful and -less. For example, the opposite of grateful isn't ~~grateless~~, but not grateful.

1 Read the Vocabulary building box. Choose the correct option to complete the sentences from the article. Use a dictionary if necessary.

1 The kayak trip was stressful / stress-free because of stormy weather.
2 I am thankful / not thankful for this amazing opportunity.
3 One careful / careless mistake could really hurt someone.
4 Working closely with students from other cultures is a great way to learn this useful / useless lesson.
5 There were moments when she felt afraid and hopeful / hopeless.

2 **PRONUNCIATION** Adjective stress

Listen to the sentences from Exercise 1. Underline the stressed syllable in each adjective. 🎧 25

3 Make two or three sentences about yourself using the words from Exercise 1. Practise saying them with the correct stress.

For me, taking exams is stressful.

READING

4 Read about scanning. Then read the sentences (1-5) about the article. Scan the article to see if the sentences are true (T) or false (F).

When you answer questions about a text, you need to find specific information. Looking through a text just for this information is called scanning. When you scan:

- focus on the information you are looking for.
- think about the type of information it is: a name, a date, a number, etc.
- let your eyes go over the text a few lines at a time. When you see useful information, stop and read closely.

1 Students in Singapore have a three- or five-day outdoor skills course as part of their education.
2 Students learn outdoor skills as a reward for their hard work on more important school subjects like maths.

'The rocks were *really* hard to grab. Then something magic happened. I climbed over the rock wall and made it! I didn't know I could make it that high.'

5 – A blogger named Singapore Student

🎧 26 In Singapore, primary and secondary school students take outdoor skills courses as part of their studies. They're usually three or five days long and include rope and rock climbing, going to sea in a
10 small boat called a kayak, sleeping in a tent each night, taking long walks in the jungle and learning to start a fire. It's real life. One careless mistake could really hurt someone. So should outdoor skills really be taught at school? Why does the Singapore
15 government think this should be part of every student's education?

Minister for Education Ng Chee Meng says that the challenge of the outdoor course helps students develop skills like critical thinking, working
20 together and good communication – abilities that are necessary for work and life. He believes that these skills are as important as traditional subjects like maths, science, literature and so on. Students need to learn from books, but for some lessons,
25 reading isn't as useful as doing.

What do the students think? 'It was so good!' said one teenager after the course. According to blogger Singapore Student, 'It makes you a more independent and caring person.' Angelique, another
30 student in Singapore, had such a good experience that she went back for a twenty-one-day course. 'It helped me to grow stronger,' she says. The kayak trip was stressful because of stormy weather. She says there were moments when she felt afraid and
35 hopeless – she thought the trip was too hard. But she remembered that 'smooth seas never made a skilled sailor' and felt brave enough to continue against the storm. 'I am thankful for this amazing opportunity, and I would do it again,' she says.

40 Right now, students attend courses with groups from their own school. After 2020, however, all students will do the course in groups from several different schools. Why does this matter? People from China, Malaysia, India and other cultures live
45 closely together in Singapore. Good communication skills are more important now than ever in order for people to live and work together. Working closely with students from other cultures is a great way to learn this useful lesson.

50 One student said it this way: 'There is nothing to be afraid of and nothing's impossible.' And that's a great lesson to learn.

3 A student named Angelique said the course was a terrible experience and she would never do it again.
4 In the future, students will take the outdoor skills course with people from other schools.
5 According to the article, one student described the course as 'impossible'.

5 Now read the article more carefully and underline the sentences that helped you do Exercise 4.

6 Work in pairs. Discuss the questions.

1 The article asks if outdoor skills should be taught at school. What do you think? Why?
2 Angelique says she felt afraid and hopeless at times, but that she would do it again. What difficult experience have you had that you learned something from?
3 In the future, students from different communities and schools will take the course together. How will difficult experiences outdoors help them learn to communicate?
4 What outdoor skills does the article mention? Which of them would you be afraid to try? Which of them do you think you would enjoy?
5 What skills does Ng Chee Meng believe students learn outdoors? Do you agree with him that they are as important as the traditional subjects? Why?

CRITICAL THINKING Analyzing quotations

7 Read the Critical thinking box. Work in pairs. Discuss the questions.

Quotations (quotes) are the original words of real people and are marked with quotation marks (Example: 'It was good,' she said). Writers use quotes to clearly show people's ideas or opinions. Writers may agree with the quotes and use them as supporting evidence, or they may argue against them. Writers sometimes use quotes from different people to show two sides of an argument.

1 How many separate quotes are used in the text?
2 What does each quote show about the outdoor skills course?
3 Why do you think the author used quotes instead of just explaining the ideas in his own words?
4 Does the article include different points of view? Why do you think the author used the quotes that are used?

8 MY PERSPECTIVE

Work in small groups. Discuss the questions.

• Would you like to learn skills like this at school? Why? / Why not?
• What do you think this kind of class could teach you about life?

Skills for life

Adults say kids today need these skills

Very important / useful
Communication
Reading

Important / useful
Maths
Working together
Writing
Logic (clear thinking)
Science

Not very important / useful
Sports
Music
Art

4C Skills for life

GRAMMAR Comparative forms

1 What can you remember about the outdoor skills course in Singapore?

- activities
- skills developed
- challenges faced by students

Comparative forms

a *Outdoor skills are **as important as** the traditional subjects.*
b *For some lessons, reading is**n't as useful as** doing.*
c *She thought the trip was **too hard**.*
d *She felt **brave enough** to continue against the storm.*
e *I wasn't **brave enough**, so I gave up.*
f *It was **so** good!*
g *Angelique had **such** a good experience.*

2 Look at the examples in the Grammar box. Match the comparative forms (a-g) with their meanings (1-6).

a *as* (adjective) *as*   4
b *not as* (adjective) *as*
c *too* (adjective)
d (adjective) *enough*
e *not* (adjective) *enough*
f *so* (adjective)
g *such a/an* (adjective + noun)

1 just the right amount
2 more than wanted/needed
3 makes something stronger
    (two examples)
4 compares two similar things
5 less than wanted/needed
6 says two things are not similar

3 Choose the correct option to complete the information about the sentences (a–g) in the Grammar box.

a Outdoor skills and traditional subjects *have / don't have* the same importance.
b For some lessons, reading and doing are *equal / not equal*.
c The trip was *the right level of difficulty / more difficult than she wanted*.
d She *had / didn't have* the right level of bravery to continue.
e I had *less / more* bravery than I needed.
f The expression ***It was so good*** is *stronger than / not as strong as* ***It was good***.
g Angelique's experience was perhaps *better / worse* than she expected.

Check your answers on page 134. Do Exercises 5–7.

4 Look at the information on the left. Then complete the sentences with (*not*) *as … as* and the adjective in brackets.

According to the research …

1 writing and maths skills are _____ (important) communication and reading skills.
2 science is _____ (useful) maths.
3 sports are _____ (useful) science.
4 communication is _____ (important) reading.
5 art is _____ (useful) working together.

5 Work in small groups. Discuss the questions about the *Skills for life* information.

- What do you think *useful* means? To whom? For what?
- Do you agree with the research? Why? / Why not? Make your own comparisons of the skills using (*not*) *as … as* sentences.

6 Choose the correct options to complete the paragraph.

Some people feel that secondary school students shouldn't study art because it (1) *is too serious / isn't serious enough* to be a real school subject. But research shows that art education is (2) *too powerful / powerful enough* to improve students' grades in their other classes. This is especially true for students who find traditional subjects (3) *too challenging / not challenging enough* to do well in. Art classes also help students connect with each other, work together and express themselves. People make similar arguments about sport. Also, although some students find sport activities (4) *too difficult / difficult enough*, having some physical exercise during the school week (5) *isn't valuable enough / is valuable enough* for schools to keep it. Those benefits are (6) *too important / important enough* to support art and sport in secondary schools.

7 Work in pairs. Discuss the questions.

- Do you agree with the paragraph in Exercise 6? Why? / Why not?
- Make sentences giving your opinion about art, sport and your other classes using *too …* and (*not*) *… enough* sentences. Use these words and other adjectives you know.

| challenging | important | interesting |
| serious | useful | |

8 Complete each sentence with *such* or *so*.

1 Music is _____ an important part of my life.
2 His experience with team sports was _____ important to him.
3 Their art class was _____ good – it made them look forward to school.
4 I had _____ a good maths teacher last year that I've decided I'd like to study maths at college.
5 Working together is _____ a useful skill that I think everyone should learn it and practise it at school.
6 The reading skills I learned made me do _____ much better in my exams.

9 Write two sentences that are true for you for each item. Share your ideas with a partner.

1 (School subject) is / isn't as (adjective) as (school subject).
   Maths is as hard as science.
2 (School subject) is too (adjective).
3 (School subject) isn't (adjective) enough.
4 My (school subject) class is so (adjective)!
5 I had such a(n) (adjective) (school subject) class that I (result).

10 CHOOSE

1 List ten skills you think students need to learn, from most to least important. Compare your list in a group. Present your group's results to the class.
2 Write a paragraph like the one in Exercise 6, saying why a skill that some people think is less important is useful.
3 Make notes about what you think the most useful skill is. Compare your skill with a partner.

Students practise in a music class.

"That child already, at four, understood the most important principle for success, which is the ability to delay gratification. "

JOACHIM DE POSADA

Read about Joachim de Posada and get ready to watch his TED Talk. ▶ **4.0**

AUTHENTIC LISTENING SKILLS

English speakers with accents

About 75% of the English spoken in the world is spoken by people who speak it as a second language. This means that you will hear many different pronunciations of both vowels and consonants. Identifying features of different accents can help you understand them more easily.

1 Read the Authentic listening skills box. Then listen to two people saying the sentence below. Notice the pronunciation of *the*. Which sentence is spoken by a Spanish speaker? Which sentence is spoken by an English speaker? 🎧 **27**

*I think we have found **the** most important factor for success.*

2 Listen to the sentences. Notice the words in bold. What's the difference between Joachim's pronunciation and the English speaker's pronunciation? 🎧 **28**

1 Johnny, I am going to leave you here with a marshmallow for fifteen **minutes**.
2 As soon as **the** door closed … two out of three ate **the** marshmallow.
3 Five **seconds**, ten **seconds**, forty **seconds**, fifty **seconds** …
4 And **they** found **that** 100 percent of the children that had not eaten the marshmallow were successful.

WATCH

3 Have you ever waited to do something? Why? What happened? Tell a partner.

4 Watch Part 1 of the talk. Complete the sentences. ▶ **4.1**

1 A researcher worked with children who were _____ years old.
2 The researcher told the children to wait for _____ minutes.
3 Children who did not eat the marshmallow would have _____ marshmallows.
4 This is the same as an adult waiting for _____ for coffee.
5 Some children lasted as long as _____ minutes before they ate the marshmallow.
6 _____ out of _____ children looked at the marshmallow and then put it back.

5 Watch Part 2 of the talk. Answer the questions. ▶ **4.2**

1 How old were the kids when the researchers met with them again?
2 How does Joachim describe the successful kids?
3 How does he describe the unsuccessful kids?
4 What country did Joachim do his next experiment in?

6 Watch Part 3 of the talk. Correct the sentences. ▶ 4.3

1 One girl in Colombia ate only the outside of the marshmallow.
2 Joachim says that she should work in a bank.
3 Joachim says that a bad salesperson asks the customer questions.
4 Joachim says that the marshmallow principle should be taught in Korea.

7 Work in pairs. Discuss the questions.

- You could say that the students who didn't eat the marshmallow followed the rules. Do you think following the rules is important? Why?
- Delaying gratification means not doing something right away. Is it sometimes necessary to do something right away and not wait? Can you give an example?

8 VOCABULARY IN CONTEXT

a Watch the clips from the talk. Choose the correct meaning of the words. ▶ 4.4

b Complete the sentences so they are true for you.
1 *One hundred percent* of my friends are …
2 *I was in trouble* when …
3 I hope I can *make it to* …
4 When I finish my education, I'd like to *go into* …
5 One thing my country *produces* is …

9 Work in pairs. Discuss the questions.

- Why does the ability to delay gratification mean you might get better grades?
- Joachim says the ability to delay gratification is the key to success. Can you think of other factors that might be important to success?
- Younger people often have to wait to do things such as drive or vote. Why is it important for people to reach a certain age before they can do these things?

CHALLENGE

Design your own experiment to test the ideas in the TED Talk. Follow these steps.

- Think about how you will ask people to delay gratification. For example, by telling them not to check their phones or not to watch a TV show right away.
- Think about how long you will ask people to delay gratification for.
- Think about what people will get if they can delay gratification for this long. For example, if students can go a whole lesson without checking their phones, they get a prize or don't have to do homework for one day.
- Share your ideas with the class and vote for the best experiment.

4E Such a cool subject!

SPEAKING

❶ MY PERSPECTIVE

Work in pairs. Discuss the questions.

- What do you think of taking classes during the school holidays? Have you done this, or would you consider it?
- What are the pros and cons of studying during school holidays?

❷ Work in pairs. Look at the list of courses. Which three look the most interesting?

- Computer skills: Create a website and learn how to write code for apps and games
- Indoor climbing: Learn climbing skills on a 15-metre climbing wall
- Science lab: Do fun and exciting experiments in the laboratory
- Art camp: Drawing, painting, photography – anything you're interested in
- Team sports: Play football, baseball, basketball and other sports
- Video-making: Write and produce short films

❸ Listen to two students talking about choosing a summer school course. Which three courses do they mention? 🎧 29

❹ Complete the sentences. Then listen again and check your answers. 🎧 29

better choice	fun enough	more interesting
most interesting	such a cool	too much like school

1 Which ones look the _____ ?
2 I'm not sure about computer skills – _____ !
3 The sports classes look _____ .
4 Do you think it's _____ for a two-week course?
5 Video-making is _____ subject.
6 That's a _____ than indoor climbing!

❺ What course do the students decide to take?

❻ Read the Useful language box. In pairs, discuss the six courses in Exercise 2 and choose one.

Useful language

Asking about opinions

Which ones look the most interesting / useful / exciting?

Is it too boring / long / expensive?

Do you think it's fun / useful / exciting enough?

Making comparisons

(The sports classes) look more interesting.

(Science lab) isn't as interesting / useful / exciting as (Art camp).

(Computer skills) looks the most interesting / useful / exciting.

Making a decision

I think (Art camp) is the best choice.

(Indoor climbing) is the most interesting.

WRITING An enquiry email

7 Read the email asking for information about a course on page 150. Tick (√) the topics you see in the email. Then number them in the correct order.

    a the reason for the email

    b the main message of the email

    c greeting   √ *1*

    d thanking the person for helping the writer

    e where the writer saw the advertisement

    f the writer's address

    g the writer's name

    h closing statement asking for a reply

    i the writer's reason for wanting to do the course

    j polite closing expression

8 **WRITING SKILL** Using polite expressions

    a Read the email on page 150 again. Underline the polite expressions in the email.

    b How could you write these expressions in an email to a friend?

9 Read the Useful language box. Use the expressions in the box and in Exercise 8 to write an email asking questions about the course you chose in Exercise 6. Use the email in Exercise 7 as a model. Make sure you use some polite expressions in your email.

10 Exchange emails with a partner. Check each other's work. Does it use the structure from Exercise 7 and the language from the Useful language box? Is it polite enough?

> ### Useful language
>
> **Saying how you know about the person or company you're writing to**
>
> *I saw your ad / website / poster.*
>
> **Saying why you're writing**
>
> *I'm writing because I'd like more information / I have some questions / I'd like to ask about …*
>
> **Saying thank you**
>
> *Thank you (in advance) for …*

High school students work on a robot that they invented in a robotics club.

5 Family and friends

A group of friends perform on a subway car in New York City, US.

5A The people in my life

VOCABULARY How's it going?

1 Look at the photo. Answer the questions.

- How would you describe these people? Do you know anyone like this?
- Why do you think they're doing this?

2 MY PERSPECTIVE

Work in pairs. Which of your friends and family are important if you want to talk about difficult things? If you need advice? If you want to have fun? If you want to learn about something?

When I need help with my homework, I usually ask my dad.

3 Copy the table below. Write the words in the correct column. Use a dictionary if necessary. Add one or two words of your own to each column.

aunt	best friend	bow	brother	classmate
cousin	friend of a friend	grandfather	grandmother	hug
kiss	neighbour	partner	say *hello*	shake hands
sister	stranger	teammate (sports)	uncle	wave

Family	Other people	Greetings

4 Follow these steps. Then compare your ideas with a partner.

1 Choose three words from the 'Family' column. Then write a definition for each family member.

Your aunt is your mother or father's sister.

2 Put the people in the 'Other people' column in order of closeness to you (1 = the closest).

3 Which greeting do you use for each person? Are there any greetings you use that aren't on the list?

I usually greet my best friend with a hug. When I meet a stranger for the first time, we usually just say hello.

5 Describe a person in your life using the following information. Can your partner guess who it is?

- male or female?
- how you greet them
- where they live
- age
- something you usually do together

A: *He's 45 years old. He lives in a town two hours from here. I usually greet him with a hug. When I see him, we usually play soccer.*
B: *Is he your cousin?*
A: *No, he isn't. My cousins are all my age.*
B: *Is he your uncle?*
A: *Yes, that's right!*

LISTENING

6 The table shows how we greet the people around us. Listen to the podcast and match each column of the table with a speaker. Write the number of the speaker at the bottom. 🎧 **30**

People	Types of greetings		
Strangers	kiss	shake hands	bow, wave
People I've met	kiss	shake hands	bow, wave
Friends	kiss and hug	wave	bow, wave
Best friends	kiss and hug	hug	bow, wave, say hello
Family	kiss and hug	shake hands, hug, kiss	show respect
Speaker			

7 Listen again. Choose the correct words. 🎧 **30**

1 In Chen's family, respect *is more important than / isn't as important as* hugs and kisses.
2 Chen's parents *talk about / show* their love with their actions.
3 Bowing is a way of showing *respect / agreement*.
4 Luiza doesn't kiss her friends when *she says hello / she's in a hurry*.
5 Luiza *kisses / doesn't kiss* her sister.
6 Hugh *hugs / doesn't hug* his cousins.
7 Hugh always shakes hands with his *teachers at school / tennis coach*.

8 Which speaker is the most like you? Copy the table in Exercise 6. Complete it with people you know and your ways of greeting them. Use the table in Exercise 6 as an example.

9 Work in small groups. Compare your tables from Exercise 8. Do you all greet people in the same way?

GRAMMAR Present perfect and past simple

10 Look at the Grammar box and read the sentences from the podcast. Match each sentence (a–d) with the best description (1–4).

Present perfect and past simple

a *I've never hugged* my dad.

b *They've given* me the things I need.

c When she first *arrived* from Japan, Yuki was uncomfortable with all the hugging and kissing.

d But she's *learned* to hug and kiss like a Brazilian now!

The sentence refers to …

1 an action in the past with a result in the present.
2 a situation that started in the past and continues to the present.
3 an experience or experiences that happened at an unspecified time.
4 a completed action that happened at a specified time in the past.

Check your answers on page 136. Do Exercises 1–4.

11 Choose the correct option to complete each sentence.

1 I *took / have taken* a few different foreign language courses.
2 Have you ever *be / been* to Brazil?
3 They've *always / ever* lived in this town.
4 *We've / We* never tried Japanese food in our lives.
5 On our holiday to India last year *we met / we've met* some interesting people.
6 I *haven't travelled / didn't travel* to many different countries.

12 Complete the text with the present perfect form of the verbs.

Photographer and anthropologist Emily Ainsworth (1) _____ (travel) the world because she wants to learn about other cultures. She (2) _____ (have) amazing experiences in many different countries, but she says Mexico is very special. 'I (3) _____ (return), and returned again,' she says, adding, 'it (4) _____ (be) my second home.' And the people (5) _____ (welcome) her – at celebrations, family events and even in a circus, where she (6) _____ (perform) as a dancer many times, and continues to do so.

13 Choose the correct options to complete the text.

Emily was sixteen when she first (1) *went / has been* to Mexico, and she (2) *went / has been* back to the country many times. Now she has a lot of friends there. During her visits, she (3) *took / has taken* pictures of Day of the Dead celebrations and many other important cultural events. At first, she just (4) *wanted / has wanted* to have photos to remember her trip. But over time, she says, she (5) *built / has built* – and continues to build – 'relationships with some really interesting people,' and wants to tell their story. As a result, she (6) *won / has won* several awards for her work.

14 PRONUNCIATION Past form endings

> There are three ways to pronounce *-ed* when it comes at the end of a past simple or past participle form: /d/ as in *tried*, /t/ as in *wished*, or /ɪd/ as in *wanted*.

a Read the Pronunciation box. Tick (√) the *-ed* pronunciation for the words in bold. Listen and check your answers. 🎧 31

	/d/	/t/	/ɪd/
1 We **celebrated** my sister's fifteenth birthday last year.			
2 My dad has **photographed** our most important family events.			
3 I've never **stayed** awake all night during the New Year celebrations.			
4 When my cousin **turned** eighteen, he had a huge party.			
5 I've never **invited** more than two or three friends to a birthday celebration.			
6 My friends and I have always **laughed** a lot at our village *fiestas*.			

b Use the words to make questions about experiences. Use the past simple or present perfect.

1 you meet anyone from another country?
2 how / you celebrate on the last day of primary school?
3 you ever go to a theme park with your friends?
4 what events / you celebrate with friends?
5 what / you do last weekend?

c Work in pairs. Ask and answer the questions in Exercise 14b.

Events like this circus in Mexico City can show what is important to a culture. When Emily joined the circus in Mexico, she learned about the people in it, as well as herself.

5B Coming of age

VOCABULARY BUILDING Suffix -al

> The suffix -al usually means related to. For example, national means related to a nation.

1 Read the sentences from the article (1–4). Match the words in bold with the correct meaning (a–d).

1 A girl's fifteenth birthday is a huge **social** occasion for many Latin American families.
2 The tradition has become **international**, spreading through Central and South America.
3 It marks a time of important **personal** change.
4 The event has both personal and **historical** importance.

Connected with …

a many countries
b the past
c a person
d groups of people

2 Complete the sentences with these adjectives.

cultural	emotional	traditional	typical

1 The *fiesta de quince años* is hundreds of years old. It's a _____ Mexican celebration.
2 Certain things are expected at most parties. At a _____ party, the girl's father removes her shoes.
3 The party brings out strong feelings. The shoe-changing can be a very _____ moment.
4 It's part of the Mexican way of life, but many countries don't have a _____ tradition like this.

3 What adjectives can you make from these nouns? Be careful. You need to remove a letter from some nouns.

centre	music	nature	politics	profession

READING

4 MY PERSPECTIVE

Work in pairs. Discuss the questions.

- What are the most important celebrations in your family?
- What do you think is the most important birthday in a person's life? Why?
- Are there any unique social celebrations in your city or country?

5 Read the article and choose the topic and main idea.

1 Topic
  a Latin American celebrations   **c** Becoming an adult
  b The *fiesta de quince años*

2 Main idea
  a The culture of ancient Mexico has affected all of Latin America.
  b The *fiesta de quince años* shouldn't be more important than a wedding.
  c A girl's fifteenth birthday is one of the most important celebrations for Latin American families.

6 Read the article again. Are the sentences true (T), false (F) or is the information not given (NG)?

1 According to the article, the biggest *fiestas de quince años* are held in Spain.
2 In the US, the *fiestas* usually aren't as big as weddings.
3 The history of the *fiesta* goes back more than 500 years.
4 There are over 500,000 *fiestas* in the US a year.
5 Some *fiestas* in the US last for a week.
6 New shoes show that the girl has become a young woman.

7 Find information in the article to support each sentence.

1 The *fiesta de quince años* is an international celebration.
2 The girl is seen as a different person after the celebration.
3 The celebrations have become bigger over time.
4 People spend a lot of money on a *fiesta de quince años*.
5 The celebration is a very old tradition.

8 Read the comments on the article. Write one of your own, making some connection with your own life or culture.

Comments

BeijingGuy Interesting post! I'm Chinese, and I've just celebrated my *Guan Li* – a twentieth birthday celebration for boys. We also celebrate a girl's fifteenth birthday. We call it *Ji Li*. Both of these are like the *fiesta de quince años* – we celebrate becoming men and women.

Agnieska In Poland, we don't have a cultural tradition like this, but for us, eighteen is a big birthday. We usually have a party with friends. You can vote and drive a car when you're eighteen. I haven't had my eighteenth birthday yet – one more year!

Haruto We have a celebration in Japan called *Seijin-no-Hi*. It's on the second Monday in January, and twenty year olds wear traditional clothes, receive gifts and have parties. My sister has already celebrated this, but I'm not old enough yet.

9 Design your perfect party. Where is it held? Who do you invite? What do you do?

A father and daughter celebrate at a *fiesta de quince años*.

From **child** to **adult** – in one day

🎧 **32** Delilah Bermejo, a New Yorker with family history in Puerto Rico and Colombia, says that 'it's the most important day' of a girl's life. The *fiesta de quince años* – a girl's fifteenth birthday celebration – is a huge social occasion for Latin American families, and is one of life's biggest celebrations. Friends and relatives come together to celebrate a girl's passing from childhood into the adult world. It marks a time of important personal change. According to Ed Hassel, manager of a company that provides food for parties in New York, the celebrations are now 'bigger than the weddings I do. We're talking 125, 150, 175 people. And they're taking Saturday night, my most expensive night.'

The event has both personal and historical importance. Families have held special celebrations for fifteen year olds for at least 500 years – since the time of the Aztecs in Mexico. At age fifteen, Aztec boys became warriors – men old enough to fight in a war – and girls became women with adult rights and duties.

In the past, parties were usually small, with a few friends and family members. It was a chance for the young woman to meet young men. Only very rich families had big *fiestas*. Since the arrival of Europeans in the Americas, the tradition has become international, spreading through Central and South America and into North America. Nowadays, big celebrations are popular with the nearly 60 million Latinos in the US and Canada.

Friends and family take an active part in a traditional Mexican *fiesta de quince años*. A 'man of honour', usually a member of the girl's family, accompanies the *quinceañera* throughout the celebration. She also chooses a 'court', often fourteen girls and fourteen boys, one for each year of her life. They stay near the *quinceañera*, join all of the dances, and look after her on her special day. The celebration often begins with a formal ceremony before it becomes a more usual birthday party with food and dancing. Families with more money usually have bigger parties. A typical ceremony ends with the girl's father removing the flat shoes that she wore to the party and replacing them with a pair of more grown-up shoes with a high heel. This can be an emotional moment. It means that the person who walked into the party as a girl leaves the party as a young woman.

Many young people celebrate *Coming of Age Day* in Japan when they turn 20.

5C Stop me if you've already heard this one

GRAMMAR Present perfect with *for*, *since*, *already*, *just* and *yet*

❶ Look at the Grammar box. Choose the correct option to complete the explanation for each sentence in the Grammar box.

> **Present perfect with *for*, *since*, *already*, *just* and *yet***
>
> **a** Families **have celebrated** the fiesta de quince años **for** about 500 years.
> **b** **Since** the arrival of Europeans in the Americas, the tradition **has become** international.
> **c** I'm Chinese, and I**'ve just celebrated** my 'Guan Li.'
> **d** I **haven't had** my eighteenth birthday **yet** – one more year.
> **e** My sister **has already celebrated** this.

    a This sentence refers to *a period of time / a certain time in the past*.
    b This sentence refers to a certain event in the *past / present* and the situation afterwards.
    c This event happened *in the recent past / a long time ago*.
    d This *has / has not* happened up to now.
    e This has happened, *but we don't know / and we know* when.

Check your answers on page 136. Do Exercises 5–8.

❷ Complete the exchanges with *for* and *since*.

    1 A: I haven't seen my cousins _____ last month.
        B: Really? I haven't seen mine _____ almost three years.
    2 A: We've been friends _____ ten years.
        B: Yeah, I guess you're right. We've known each other _____ we were five years old.
    3 A: Has your brother been in the running club _____ long?
        B: Not really. He's been a member _____ January.

❸ Complete the questions with *you* and the correct form of verbs in brackets. Then work in pairs to answer each question with *for* and *since*.

    1 How long _____ (know) your best friend?
    2 How long _____ (live) in the home you now live in?
    3 How long _____ (study) English?
    4 How long _____ (attend) the school you go to now?

❹ Complete the text with *just*, *already* or *yet*.

'Comedy is kind of a language, so you're connected and relating.' – Gad Elmaleh

Moroccan-born comedian Gad Elmaleh has taken a lot of English lessons in his life, but jokes that he doesn't really speak English (1) _____ . However, that hasn't stopped him from performing comedy for American audiences. Although he arrived in the US fairly recently, he's (2) _____ done shows in New York, Los Angeles and lots of cities in between. He's (3) _____ completed a tour of more than ten US cities, and plans to continue performing.

Although Gad has (4) _____ started his comedy career in America, he's (5) _____ a superstar in Europe – especially France. In the US, he hasn't become that popular (6) _____ . His career, like his English, is a work in progress.

5 Put the words in the correct place in each sentence.

1 A: I've heard a really funny joke. (just) Why is *U* the happiest letter?

2 B: Because it's in the middle of *fun*. Sorry, but I've heard that one! (already)

3 A: OK, here's one you probably haven't heard. (yet) Why is six afraid of seven?

4 B: Because seven ate nine! My brother has told me that one! (already)

6 Answer the questions. Use the present perfect.

1 What have you done recently that you're proud of?

My homework is due next week, and I've already finished writing it.
I've just passed my grade 3 piano test.

2 What have you done for a long time that you're proud of?

I've been on the football team for five years.
I've taken art classes on Saturdays since I was eleven years old.

3 What haven't you done yet, but would like to do?

I haven't learned to play a musical instrument yet, but I'd like to.
I haven't read a novel in English yet, but I want to read one.

7 CHOOSE

1 Work in pairs. Tell your partner about the things you wrote about in Exercise 6. Ask and answer questions.

A: *How long have you played the piano?*
B: *Since I was about five years old.*
A: *Does anyone else in your family play?*
B: *Yes, my mother plays, and my brother does, too.*

2 Write a paragraph about one of the things you wrote about in Exercise 6. Give more information about it.

3 Prepare a short presentation about one of the things you wrote about in Exercise 6. Tell the class about it.

Birthday celebrations are important get-togethers for many families around the world. This family is celebrating in Brazil.

> **" You are laughing to show people that you understand them, that you agree with them, that you're part of the same group as them. "**
>
> **SOPHIE SCOTT**

Read about Sophie Scott and get ready to watch her TED Talk. ▶ **5.0**

AUTHENTIC LISTENING SKILLS

Dealing with fast speech

Some people speak very quickly, often because they are excited about a topic or they are nervous. Here are some ways to deal with fast speech:

- Listen for words or ideas that the speaker repeats.
- Try to get an idea of the main idea and then connect it with what you hear.
- Focus on what you *do* understand and try not to worry too much about what you don't understand.

❶ Read the Authentic listening skills box. Then listen to the first part of the TED Talk and answer the questions. 🎧 **33**

1 What words or ideas does the speaker repeat?
2 What words tell us that she's talking about her childhood?
3 In your own words, say what you think she's describing.

❷ Listen again. What is the point of Sophie's story? 🎧 **33**

a When she was a child, she usually didn't understand her parents' jokes.
b When we hear people laughing, we want to laugh with them.
c Sometimes, laughing can make the people around you feel bad.

WATCH

❸ Watch Part 1 of the talk. Are the sentences true (T) or false (F)? ▶ **5.1**

1 Sophie's parents were laughing at a song.
2 The first recording includes both a man and an animal.
3 Sophie is worried that the second person laughing doesn't breathe in.
4 The third recording is an example of a monkey laughing, which is very similar to a human.

❹ Watch Part 2 of the talk. Choose the correct option to complete each sentence. ▶ **5.2**

1 People laugh mostly when
  a they hear a joke.   c they're with friends.
  b they watch a comedy.
2 When we hear other people laugh, we usually
  a start laughing.   c think they're laughing at us.
  b ask why they're laughing.
3 Laughter that we cannot control is called _____ laughter.
  a voluntary   c vocal
  b involuntary
4 We can choose to laugh when we want to be _____ to another person.
  a horrible   c polite
  b funny
5 The first recording is _____ laughter.
  a polite   c not really
  b involuntary
6 The second recording is _____ laughter.
  a polite   c not really
  b involuntary

5 Complete the summary of Part 3 of the talk before you watch it. Then watch it and check your answers. ▶ 5.3

animals   bonds   emotions   humans   laughs   sounds

(1) _____ are not the only (2) _____ that laugh – many mammals laugh to feel better. And animals also have both real and fake (3) _____ with very different (4) _____ . Laughter helps us maintain social (5) _____ and control our (6) _____ .

6 **VOCABULARY IN CONTEXT**

a Watch the clips from the talk. Choose the correct meaning of the words and phrases. ▶ 5.4

b Complete the sentences with your own words. Then discuss with a partner.

1 I think … is *weird*.
2 I had an *odd* experience when …
3 I think … is *silly*.
4 I would like to know more about the *origins* of …
5 I would like to know the *roots* of …

CRITICAL THINKING Recognize supporting evidence

> Speakers often give evidence to support their theory or idea. Evidence may include images, recordings, demonstrations, or quotations from experts or other reliable people.

7 Read the Critical thinking box. Work in pairs. How does this evidence from the talk support Sophie Scott's message that 'laughter is an ancient behaviour that we use to benefit ourselves and others in complex and surprising ways.'

1 She plays examples of real human beings laughing and asks us to think about how primitive laughter is as a sound.
2 She points out that the audience laughed when listening to others laugh.
3 She plays recordings of voluntary and involuntary laughter.

8 Work in pairs. Discuss the questions.

- Which part of Sophie's talk was the most interesting to you? Why?
- Have your ideas about laughter changed? How?

CHALLENGE
For a couple of days, listen for people laughing. Try to notice examples of both real and polite laughter. Make notes. Present your results to the class, explaining the situations where you heard each type of laughter.

9 Work in groups. Discuss the questions.

- Sophie says that we laugh 'to show people that you understand them, that you agree with them, that you're part of the same group as them.' What other ways do we show that we are part of the group?
- Most people are part of more than one group. How many groups are people in at in your school?
- How do the people in the groups you named above show that they are part of that group?

5E Invitations

Asking if someone is available

Are you busy next Saturday?

Are you around / free on Sunday?

Are you doing anything on Tuesday night?

Saying if you are available or not

I (don't) think so.

It depends.

I'm not sure.

I'll have to ask my parents.

I need to check my schedule.

Accepting an invitation

Sure, I'd love to.

That sounds great!

Saying *no* to an invitation

Thanks for inviting me, but I'm afraid I'm busy.

Sorry, I can't make it. But thank you for inviting me.

SPEAKING

1 MY PERSPECTIVE

How do you think the students in the photo feel? Why? What exactly has happened?

2 Listen to the conversation. What important life event is mentioned? 🎧 **34**

3 Listen again. Tick (√) the things the students have done. Then discuss them. 🎧 **34**

1 order the food and drinks
2 sort out the music
3 send out the invitations
4 buy the balloons
5 decorate the room
6 schedule a meeting with Davina

They've ordered the food and drinks, but …

4 You're having a party to welcome a new student, Delia, to your school. Decide on a day, time, location and type of food for it.

5 Work in pairs. Take turns to invite each other and saying whether you can or can't go. Use expressions from the Useful language box.

WRITING Informal invitations and replies

6 Read the three notes on page 150. Match each one with the correct purpose.

1 making an invitation
2 saying no to an invitation
3 accepting an invitation

7 In each note, underline the expressions used for making, accepting or saying *no* to an invitation.

8 In informal notes, we sometimes use abbreviations. Find an abbreviation in each note. Which one means the following?

1 Let me know if you can come.
2 as soon as possible
3 I also want to say …

9 **WRITING SKILL** Politely making and replying to invitations

Work in pairs. Read the Writing strategies box. Together, write one sentence inviting someone to a celebration, write one sentence accepting and one sentence saying *no*.

10 Think of a celebration you would like to have. Write an informal invitation to your partner. Use two abbreviations.

11 Exchange invitations. Then write a reply to your partner's invitation.

12 Check each other's work. Do the notes use abbreviations and the Writing strategies correctly?

Politely making and replying to invitations

- When you write an invitation, give the time, date, location and type of event. Remember to ask the person to let you know if they can come.

- When you accept an invitation, begin by saying *thank you*. If you have any questions about the event, ask them. It can be polite to offer to bring something (food or drinks, for example).

- When you say *no* to an invitation, begin by saying *thank you*. Apologize that you can't make it, and say why – without giving too many details if you don't want to. It can be polite to end by saying you hope they enjoy the event and offering to make plans another time.

Students in Punjab, India, celebrate their graduation.

6 Do your best

6A The best I can be

VOCABULARY Goals and expectations

1 Look at the photo. Many of the tiles used are broken or come from people's rubbish. Do you still think the stairs are beautiful?

2 Match the words in bold (1–7) with the correct definitions (a–g).

1 'I have not **failed**. I've just found several thousand ways that won't work.'
– Thomas Edison
2 'The only place where **success** comes before work is in the dictionary.'
– Anonymous
3 'Have no fear of **perfection**; you'll never reach it.' – Salvador Dali
4 'Beauty is about being comfortable in your own skin. It's about knowing and **accepting** who you are.' – Ellen DeGeneres
5 'Practice makes **perfect**.' – Anonymous
6 'Practice doesn't make perfect. Practice reduces the **imperfection**.'
– Toba Beta
7 'True success is overcoming the fear of being **unsuccessful**.' – Paul Sweeney

a having no mistakes or problems (n)
b finished without success (v)
c without mistakes (adj)
d the correct or wanted result (n)
e not getting the correct or wanted result (adj)
f not being exactly right (n)
g feeling that something is OK or normal (v)

3 Choose the correct option to complete the meaning of each quotation in Exercise 2.

1 When you find a way that doesn't work, you learn something new. When you learn nothing, you *fail / succeed*.
2 You *don't have to / have to* work before you can succeed.
3 Perfection is a nice idea, *and we should / but we shouldn't* expect to reach it.
4 Beauty isn't about how you look, it's about *how you feel / dressing comfortably*.
5 If you want to do something really well, *you won't fail / practise a lot*.
6 You can never be perfect, *but you can / and you can't* usually improve.
7 Success means not being afraid of *other people / failure*.

4 Match the words on the left (1–6) with their opposites (a–f). Use a dictionary if necessary.

1 perfection   a unsuccessful
2 success   b fail
3 perfect   c imperfect
4 succeed   d imperfection
5 accept   e reject
6 successful   f failure

5 MY PERSPECTIVE

Work in pairs. Discuss the questions.

- Have you ever failed? What did you do next? Do you think failure can lead to success?
- Have you ever seen or experienced something that was perfect? What was it?
- Can something be 'too perfect?' Why?

The Selaron Steps in Rio de Janeiro, Brazil, are made from pieces of tile found in the city and donated from around the world.

LISTENING

6 Work in pairs. Discuss the questions.

- Can you think of a food that doesn't look good but tastes delicious?
- Have you eaten had a food that looked perfect but didn't taste very good?
- Have you ever been surprised by a food or drink? For example, something that looked sweet but tasted spicy?

7 Listen to a podcast about a fruit and vegetable seller in Tokyo. Are the sentences true (T) or false (F)? Rewrite the false sentences. 🎧 35

1 Senbikiya is a small grocery shop in Tokyo.
2 Senbikiya isn't very successful because it's too expensive.
3 In Japan, fruit is a popular gift because it is something you don't need.
4 In Japan, giving fruit as a gift started recently.
5 The carrots on this page probably don't come from Senbikiya.

8 Listen to a podcast about a fruit and vegetable seller in France. Choose the correct option to complete each sentence. 🎧 36

1 Intermarché sells fruit and vegetables that are
  a ugly and popular.   **c** ugly and not popular.
  b perfect but not popular.

2 Customers like Intermarché's fruit and vegetables because of the
  a funny way they look.   **c** taste and price.
  b price alone.

3 In the past, most 'ugly' fruit and vegetables were
  a given to animals.   **c** sold to supermarkets.
  b thrown away.

4 Rejecting imperfect fruit and vegetables _____ food.
  a wastes   **c** improves the flavour of
  b lowers the price of

5 Now, _____ are choosing to eat imperfect fruit and vegetables.
  a only very hungry people   **c** more people
  b most farmers

9 MY PERSPECTIVE

Work in pairs. Discuss the questions.

- Do you think Senbikiya and Intermarché would be successful in your country? Why? / Why not?
- Which shop would you prefer: Senbikiya or Intermarché? Why?
- Are there any interesting shops like this where you live?
- Is fruit a luxury in your country, or would it be a very strange gift?
- Does it matter if vegetables and fruit don't look perfect? Why? / Why not?

10 CHOOSE

1 Think of products other than food where a perfect appearance is important. Make a list of three or four things. Then think of products where an imperfect appearance is acceptable. Make a list of three or four things. Compare your lists with a partner.

  Perfect appearance important: *new cars,*

  Imperfect appearance acceptable: *soap,*

2 Work in pairs. Make a list of situations when a person's appearance is important. When do people dress nicely and try to look as perfect as possible?

3 Work in small groups. Think about how people present themselves on social media. Do you think people try to present themselves as more perfect and successful than they are in real life? Do you feel pressure to do this?

Look at these carrots. Do you think they still taste normal?

GRAMMAR Modal verbs: obligation, prohibition, permission, advice

11 Answer the questions about presenting yourself online.

1 What social media sites and apps do you use?
2 What kind of photos of yourself do you put online?
3 How do people use social media to make their lives look more interesting than they are? Do you do this?

12 Read the article about social media. What is it important to do? What is it important not to do?

Rules for the perfect profile?

According to the rules, you have to be at least thirteen years old to open an account on Instagram, Facebook, Snapchat and other social media apps, but of course anyone eighteen or over can join. Although the rules say younger kids can't join, you don't have to prove your age, so a lot of them still join. This worries some experts. Research shows that the 'perfect lives' kids see on social media can cause them to feel bad about their own lives. Parents should explain to kids that what people show online isn't the whole picture, and they mustn't take it too seriously. The Imperfect Tribe, a group that started on Instagram, agrees. They say we shouldn't try to look perfect on social media. In fact, members of the group must show themselves as real people online.

Modal verbs

Obligation
a *You **have to** be at least thirteen to open an account.*
b *Members of the group **must** show themselves as real people online.*

Prohibition
c *The rules say younger kids **can't** join.*
d *They **mustn't** take it too seriously.*

Permission
e *Anyone eighteen or over **can** join.*

Lack of obligation
f *You **don't have to** prove your age.*

Advice
g *Parents **should** explain to kids that what people show online isn't the whole picture.*
h *They say we **shouldn't** try to look perfect …*

---

13 Look at the examples in the Grammar box. Match the examples with the correct meanings (1–6).

1 It would be a good idea to do this.
2 It would be a good idea **not** to do this.
3 You are allowed to do this.
4 You are **not** allowed to do this. (two examples)
5 It is necessary to do this. (two examples)
6 It isn't necessary to do this.

Check your answers on page 138. Do Exercises 1–4.

14 Choose the correct options to complete the quotes about school uniforms.

'We have a strict uniform policy at my school. Boys
(1) *have to / can't* wear black trousers, but girls
(2) *shouldn't / can* choose a skirt or trousers. Girls' skirts
(3) *can't / must* touch the top of their knees. You
(4) *can't / don't have to* loosen your tie at school during the day, and girls (5) *have to / mustn't* let their socks fall down.' – Park, Korea

'We don't have a uniform, so we (6) *can't / don't have to* wear a tie or jacket. We (7) *can / should* wear mostly what we like, though we (8) *have to / mustn't* come to school in beach clothes or something like that. The rules aren't specific, but they say we (9) *mustn't / should* look neat.'
– Sofia, Italy

15 Work in pairs. Are there rules about how to dress at your school? What advice would you give a new student about what to wear?

16 Complete the rules with these words.

can	can't	have to	must	should

Dressing for the temples of Thailand

Visitors to Thailand (1) _____ visit the amazing temples. But there are some rules you (2) _____ follow to be respectful. First, you (3) _____ wear shoes in the temples. Second, you (4) _____ wear clothes that cover your arms and knees. But in most temples there are no rules about covering your head – you (5) _____ enter without a hat or headscarf.

17 PRONUNCIATION Reduced *have to* and *has to*

Read about how we say *have to* and *has to*. Then read and listen to the conversation. Underline the reduced forms. 🎧 37

> When talking about obligation, people don't usually stress *has to* and *have to* when they are in the middle of a sentence. They also usually connect the words. At the end of a clause, or when an obligation is emphasized, *has to* and *have to* are stressed.

A: Does your football team have to wear a suit and tie on game day?
B: We don't have to, but we want to. We want to look our best.
A: But everyone has to wear the official uniform to play, right?
B: Yes, everyone has to. It's a rule.

18 Work in pairs. Discuss the questions.

• When in your life have you had to wear certain clothes for a special event, job or activity?
• How should people dress for an important event like a college interview?

Not so fast

Lewis Pugh swims in Lake Imja, Mount Everest.

VOCABULARY BUILDING Negative prefixes

> A prefix can be added to the beginning of a word to change its meaning. Some prefixes give words the opposite meaning, for example:
> *im-* (*imperfect* = not perfect)
> *dis-* (*disagree* = not agree)
> *un-* (*unsuccessful* = not successful)
> *in-* (*informal* = not formal)

1 Work in pairs. Read the Vocabulary building box. Then complete the words below with *im-*, *dis-*, *in-* or *un-*. Use a dictionary if necessary.

Why being comfortable can be bad for your career
CEO Kathy Bloomgarden says that if you want to succeed, you need to be (1) _un_comfortable. She believes that it's (2) _____possible to grow unless you have challenges. She realized that only speaking one language was a (3) _____advantage in business, so she learned Arabic and Chinese.

Why being patient may not help you learn a new language
Blogger Benny Lewis believes that the best way to learn a language is to be (4) _____patient. If you really want to succeed, you must be (5) _____able to wait. He says that if you just start talking to people, your fear will (6) _____appear. And talking to people is an (7) _____expensive way to learn!

2 Complete the sentences so they are true for you. Share your ideas with a partner.

1 I feel *comfortable / uncomfortable* when …
I feel comfortable when I'm relaxing with my friends.

2 For me, it would be *possible / impossible* to …
3 One *advantage / disadvantage* of the place I live is …
4 I feel *successful / unsuccessful* when …
5 I'm usually *able / unable* to …
6 Something I would like to see *appear / disappear* is …
7 For me, it's *perfect / imperfect* that …
8 I *agree / disagree* with …

READING

3 Work with a partner. Look at the photo and the caption. Discuss the questions.

1 Where is this person? What is he doing?
2 How do you think he feels?
3 Would you ever try something like this? Why? / Why not?

4 Read the article. Answer the questions.

1 Why does Lewis swim?
2 Where did he do a high-altitude swim?
3 What style of swimming was successful for him for most of his career?
4 What style of swimming was successful for the Lake Imja swim?
5 What lesson did Lewis learn through failure?

What are you really good at? What would you do if all of a sudden you failed at it? For 'pioneer swimmer' and National Geographic Adventurer of the Year Lewis Pugh, swimming has
5 been a way to share his passion for the environment with the world. He has swum in every ocean in the world and in some dangerous places where people thought swimming would be impossible.

He swims to raise awareness for issues like global
10 warming, but the swims often take place in extremely cold temperatures. After one scary and dangerous swim at the North Pole, Lewis reached a conclusion: no more cold-water swimming.

But in 2010, he heard about the snow disappearing
15 from the Himalayas and wanted to tell the world about it. He made the decision to swim two kilometres (1.2 miles) across Lake Imja, a very cold lake near Mount Everest, at 5,300 metres (17,388 feet) above sea level.

20 On his first attempt, he failed. Unable to breathe normally at the high altitude*, he almost drowned. The experience was frightening.

However, Pugh learned something. He usually swims as fast as possible, fighting against the water. After all,
25 don't all athletes try to be the fastest? But that was a disadvantage at high altitude. Members of his team said that he must forget everything he knew about swimming and swim slowly. Instead of struggling against the water, he must stay relaxed and move
30 easily through it.

Two days after his near-death experience, Pugh returned to the lake for another try. He remained calm and slowly swam across it successfully. From his failure, he learned an important lesson: if at first you
35 don't succeed, try something different – especially when you think you already know everything.

altitude *how high something is above the level of the sea*

See the TED Talk by Lewis Pugh 'How I swam the North Pole', in Perspectives Intermediate, Unit 3.

5 Read about cause and effect. Then read the article again and match the causes (1–4) with the effects (a–d).

> Readings often present causes and effects – events that lead to other situations or results. Understanding cause and effect can help you understand how the ideas in the reading are connected.

1 Lewis was afraid.
2 Lewis wanted people to know about global warming.
3 Lewis failed to swim across Lake Imja.
4 Lewis changed his swimming style.

a He went swimming near Mount Everest.
b He decided he wouldn't swim in cold water ever again.
c He succeeded in swimming across Lake Imja.
d He changed his swimming style.

6 Match the pairs of synonyms from the article.

1 conclusion (line 12)   **a** scary (line 11)
2 frightening (line 22)   **b** decision (line 16)
3 fight (line 24)   **c** attempt (line 20)
4 try (line 32)   **d** struggle (line 28)
5 calm (line 33)   **e** relaxed (line 29)

CRITICAL THINKING Making inferences

> Inference helps readers understand a meaning that isn't directly stated. For example, the article tells us that Lewis did two very difficult swims. It doesn't say directly that he's a strong swimmer, but we can make the inference that he must be a strong swimmer or he could not do those difficult swims.

7 Read the Critical thinking box. Then choose the word in each pair of opposites that best describes Lewis's style of swimming and personality. Use a dictionary if necessary.

1 lazy   hard-working
2 confident   shy
3 successful unsuccessful
4 afraid   brave
5 weak   strong

8 For each answer you gave in Exercise 7, underline the information in the article that supports your answer.

9 Make a list of other words to describe Lewis based on what you know from the article. Use a dictionary if necessary. Compare your list with a partner and discuss any differences.

10 MY PERSPECTIVE

Work in groups. What do you think about Lewis's extreme swimming? Is it brave to do something like that for a good cause? Or is it too dangerous?

6C Unexpected art

GRAMMAR Zero conditional

1 Work in pairs. Answer the questions.

- What do you really enjoy doing for fun?
- Can you imagine a job that would pay you to do something you love?

> **Zero conditional**
>
> *When you **do** what you love, you **love** what you do.*
> *If you **don't risk** failure, you **can't succeed**.*
> *When you **make** mistakes, you **can learn** a lot.*

2 Look at the examples in the Grammar box. Then answer the questions.

1 In each sentence, what verb tense is used in the *if* or *when* clause?
2 What verb tense is used in the result clause of each sentence?

Check your answers on page 138. Do Exercises 5–8.

3 Complete the article with these clauses. Write the correct letter (a-f).

- **a** you travel to New York
- **b** you aren't stopped from painting on walls
- **c** it doesn't feel like work
- **d** people want to buy an artist's work
- **e** if you work hard
- **f** art galleries can sell it

When you love your job, (1) __c__ . That's definitely the case with street artist Lady Aiko. If (2) _____ , you may see her work on buildings – and in art galleries. Some street artists have to work in secret, but when your work is as good as Lady Aiko's, (3) _____ . In fact, you can get paid to paint on them. And if a street artist's work becomes popular, (4) _____ . When (5) _____ , the artist is doing something right. Lady Aiko is successful because of bravery and persistence. When she started out, most street artists were men, and people were surprised to see a woman street artist. Lady Aiko shows that (6) _____ , you can change people's expectations.

> **Zero conditional to give advice**
>
> *If you **love** street art, **go** to Rio de Janeiro.*
> *When you **go**, **visit** the Selaron Steps.*
> *If you **visit** the Selaron Steps, you **should take** a lot of photos.*

4 Look at the examples in the Grammar box. Then answer the questions.

1 In each sentence, what verb tense is used in the *if* or *when* clause?
2 What verb form is used in the result clause when we give advice?

5 Cross out one incorrect word in each piece of advice for artists.

1 If you want to be an artist, ~~should~~ do it – just start painting.
2 When you aren't sure what to do, you should to just keep painting – don't stop.
3 If when you want to grow as an artist, you should look at other people's work.
4 When you are ready for people to see your work, if you can put your photos on the internet.
5 When you feel like you're failing, if try to learn from the experience.

Lady Aiko painted this image in Dubai in 2016.

6 Choose the correct options to complete the article.

Escadaria Selarón

If you (1) *go / will go* to Rio de Janeiro, Brazil, you (2) *visit / should visit* the Escadaria Selarón – the Selaron Steps. Artist Jorge Selarón started work on the steps as a hobby in 1990, but soon learned that if you (3) *love / should love* something, it can become your life's work. Before starting the steps, Selarón was a struggling painter. But soon, the steps became popular with both locals and tourists. When you first see the steps, you immediately (4) *notice / noticed* a lot of green, yellow, and blue – the colours of the Brazilian flag. According to Selarón, originally from Chile, the steps are his gift to the people of Brazil. When you (5) *can look / look* closely, you can see hundreds of words and pictures in the tiles. Selarón said that each tile tells a story. If that's true, then the stairs, made with four thousand tiles, (6) *had / have* four thousand stories to tell.

7 Complete the sentences with one word from the box in each space.

If	like	should	try	When	work

1 If you _____ street art, you should look for Lady Aiko's work.

2 _____ street artists become famous, they can make a lot of money.

3 If you _____ hard at something, your ability usually improves.

4 When you fail, _____ to learn from it.

5 _____ an artist wants a bigger audience, they can put their artwork on the internet.

6 When you find something you love doing, you _____ make time for it.

8 **PRONUNCIATION** Conditional intonation

Read about intonation in conditional sentences. Then listen and mark the upward and downward intonation on the sentences in Exercise 7. 🎧 **39**

In conditional sentences that begin with *If* or *When*, the intonation often rises on the *if/when* clause and falls on the result clause.

If you're interested in art, you should visit the Selaron Steps.

When visitors come to town, we like to show them the sights.

9 Listen to the sentences in Exercise 7 again. Then practise saying the sentences with natural conditional intonation. 🎧 **39**

10 **CHOOSE**

1 Tourists enjoy seeing the work of Lady Aiko in New York and Jorge Selarón in Rio de Janeiro. Work in pairs. Think of things in your country that tourists enjoy seeing. Tell people to see them using zero conditional sentences. Then present your work to another pair.

When you visit our city, you should see …

2 Exercise 5 gives tips for street artists. Think of something you know about – learning a language, doing a sport, taking photographs – and write tips for doing it. Use zero conditional sentences.

When you want to learn photography, you should start by …

3 Jorge Selarón used broken tiles to create beauty. Think of a place in your area that isn't beautiful. Imagine how you could use recycled materials to make it beautiful. Make a poster showing your ideas and explaining the improvement. Use zero conditional sentences.

When an area is ugly and dirty, people don't go there. When you make it beautiful, …

This painting is from the Bowery Wall, New York, 2012.

Teach girls bravery, not perfection

" We have to show them that they will be loved and accepted not for being perfect but for being courageous. "

RESHMA SAUJANI

Read about Reshma Saujani and get ready to watch her TED Talk. ▶ **6.0**

AUTHENTIC LISTENING SKILLS

Contrast

A **contrast** is when a speaker shows that two ideas, facts, or situations are different. Words such as *but* and *however* often mark contrasts. A speaker may also change their tone to mark contrast.

1 Read the Authentic listening skills box. Match the contrasting ideas in the extracts from the TED Talk.

1 She tried, she came close, but
2 She'll think that her student spent the past twenty minutes just staring at the screen. But
3 Girls are really good at coding, but
4 We have to begin to undo the socialization of perfection, but
5 This was my way to make a difference … The polls, however,

a if she presses 'undo' a few times, she'll see that her student wrote code and then deleted it.
b we've got to combine it with building a sisterhood* that lets girls know that they are not alone.
c it's not enough just to teach them to code.
d she didn't get it exactly right.
e told a very different story.

sisterhood *a group of girls or women who work together and help each other*

2 Listen to the extracts and check your answers to Exercise 1. 🎧 **40**

WATCH

3 Work in pairs. Discuss the questions before you watch the talk.

- Is perfection always better or more useful than imperfection? Why / Why not?
- Is it more important to be perfect or to try new things? Why / Why not?
- Can always wanting to be perfect make a person not try new things? Why / Why not? Has this ever happened to you?

4 Watch Part 1 of the talk. Choose the correct option to complete each sentence. ▶ **6.1**

1 Reshma started her career working in
  a politics.
  b banking.
  c marketing.

2 She wanted to have a more active role in government to
  a make more money.
  b change things.
  c raise money for others.

3 She tried for an elected job in government
  a and won.
  b but changed her mind.
  c and lost badly.

4 She tells the story about running for government to show that
  a she was perfect.
  b she was brave for the first time.
  c she was always brave.

5 Watch Part 2 of the talk. Answer the questions. ▶ 6.2

1 What does Reshma say that boys are rewarded for, but girls are taught to avoid?
2 What does she feel that girls lack?
3 What do students need to accept when they are learning to code?
4 What do girls often think if they have problems with their code?
5 According to Reshma, why do girls often not answer questions?
6 According to Reshma, when should we teach girls to be brave?

6 **VOCABULARY IN CONTEXT**

a Watch the clips from the TED Talk. Choose the correct meanings of the words. ▶ 6.3

b Work in pairs. Discuss the questions.

1 Think of a time when you had to be *courageous*. What happened?
2 Have you ever *run* for a position, for example, captain of a sports team? What was it? What would you like to *run* for?
3 What kind of things do you *negotiate* with your parents? With your teachers?
4 Have you ever seen a person's *supportive network* in action? What was the reason?
5 Do you think everyone has the *potential* to do something good or brave? What do you have the *potential* to do?
6 Is there anything that you have to *struggle* to achieve? What?

7 Think of something you have learned to do – speak a language, play a musical instrument, play a sport or something else. Make notes.

• What was the skill or activity?
• What challenges did you face? How did you have to be brave to continue learning?
• What kind of mistakes did you make while learning it?
• What advice would you give to someone learning the activity?

8 Work in small groups. Discuss your activity from Exercise 7.

CHALLENGE

Work in groups. Discuss the questions.

• Writing code is a process of trial and error and requires perseverance. What other activities require trial and error and perseverance?
• Reshma says in her talk that a supportive network is an important part of learning. Have you ever had a supportive network? Who was in it?
• Can you think of a time when you did something – even something small or simple – that felt brave? What did you learn from it?
• The journalist Arianna Huffington said, 'Failure is not the opposite of success, but a stepping stone to success.' Do you agree or disagree? Why?
• In your country, where are girls and women underrepresented and why?
• Reshma talks about the ways that boys are socialized. Is this also harmful to society? Does it limit the opportunities for boys? If so, how?

6E Giving advice

SPEAKING

1 Work in pairs. Discuss the questions.

- Who do you usually ask for advice? Why?
- Have you ever given advice? What about?

2 Read the question and advice. What word do you think is missing?

> ### Q&A
>
> **SS** **Sam S:** My friend is good at _____ , but won't speak in class or use her _____ because she's afraid of making a mistake. She wants her _____ to be perfect. What should I say to her?
>
> **AP** **Ania P:** If she wants to speak _____ , she should just start speaking _____ . Nobody notices mistakes.
>
> **SR** **Sixtos R:** She should learn to love mistakes. The only way to improve is to make mistakes, especially when you have a teacher there to correct you.
>
> **RD** **Ryuji D:** Why not start an _____ film club? When you watch a film, you naturally want to talk about it. You could have an '_____-only' rule for the club.
>
> **IM** **Igor M:** I agree that she shouldn't worry about mistakes, just keep trying. If you want to improve your _____ , try speaking it often.

3 Work in pairs. Discuss the questions.

1 Which advice do you think is the most helpful?
2 Can you think of other advice that would be useful for improving your English?
3 Have you ever heard any advice for speaking English that didn't work for you?

4 Look at the Useful language box. Work in small groups and take turns giving advice for these situations.

1 You can see that someone is trying to work out where to put the coins in a drinks machine. You know the correct place to put them in.
2 A friend asks you what kind of phone you think they should buy.
3 You notice that someone in a shop is having problems carrying their items. They probably don't realize that the shop has baskets they can use.

Useful language

Requested advice

When you don't understand something in class, you should ask your teacher for help.

If you need more maths practice, try downloading a maths app.

Why don't you …

Uninvited advice

If the computer isn't working, you might want to try restarting it.

I can see you don't have a phone signal. I got a signal near the window, and that may work for you.

I'm not sure, but I think this door is locked after 6:00. You may/might need to use the side entrance.

WRITING An advice blog

5 Work in pairs. Discuss the questions.

- How do you prepare for exams?
- How do you feel before or during exams? Do you often feel worried or stressed?
- What do you do to reduce your worry or stress?

6 Read the advice blog on page 151. Answer the questions.

1 What problem does the blog talk about?
2 How many solutions does the blog give?
3 Have you used any of these tips? If so, which ones?
4 Which tip do you think is the most useful?

7 Read the Writing strategies box. Does the blog on page 151 include all of the information mentioned in the box?

8 Choose one of the problems. Ask your classmates for possible solutions.

- You are often late meeting friends, arriving at school, etc.
- You spend too much time on social media when you should be studying.
- You have too many activities – sports, music, etc. You enjoy them all, but you're too busy.

9 Work in pairs. Choose one of the problems from Exercise 7b and think of a different problem of your own. Discuss the questions. Make notes of your answers.

1 What exactly is the problem? Give details.
2 Why is it a problem? Give two or three reasons.
3 What are the possible solutions? Think of at least three or four.

10 **WRITING SKILL** Giving advice

Look at the advice blog on page 151 again. What are the three ways of giving advice in the solutions?

11 Write a short blog in your pairs about your problem and three to five possible solutions. Use this structure.

1 Introduce the topic.
2 Say what the problem is.
3 Say why it's a problem.
4 Offer three to five solutions.
5 Give a conclusion.

12 Work with another pair. Exchange your blogs and check each other's work. Does it answer the questions in the Writing strategies box? Does it use the structures for giving advice?

> ### Writing strategies
>
> **Explaining problems and solutions**
>
> A problem-solution paragraph usually begins with a sentence that introduces the topic. Then it answers these questions.
>
> - What is the problem?
> - Why is it a problem?
> - What is the solution / are the solutions?
>
> It will then often include a concluding sentence.

7 Tell me what you eat

7A Food and flavours from around the world

VOCABULARY Food, drink and flavours

1 Work in pairs. Discuss the questions.

- What's your favourite food? Would you like the food in the photo?
- Is there any food you really don't like? What is it? Why don't you like it?

2 Match each food or drink with a type and a flavour. (Two don't match with a flavour.) Use a dictionary if necessary.

Food / Drink	Type	Flavour
chilli powder	fruit	salty
lemon	vegetable	sweet
coffee	meat	sour
strawberry	spice	bitter
potato crisps	drink	spicy
tomato	dessert	
ice cream	snack	
beef		

3 Think of at least one more food or drink for each of the five flavours. Make a list.

4 Match the food or drink (1–8) with the best description (a–f). Two do not have a description.

1 curry		**5** pasta
2 french fries		**6** tea
3 prawns		**7** tomato
4 ice cream		**8** apple

a Most people think of this food as Italian, but many experts think it probably came from Chinese noodles originally.

b This is a spicy food originally from India. The strong flavour comes from the hot pepper and other spices that cooks use.

c Many people think this red fruit is a vegetable, because it is often used in salads or salty sauces. People in Mexico first grew and ate it more than 2,000 years ago.

d Like coffee, this drink is bitter. People often add sugar to make it sweet. People in China were probably the first to drink it, but now it's popular around the world.

e This salty food is similar to chips. People eat it as a snack or with a meal. No one is sure, but it may come from Belgium.

f This dessert often comes in sweet fruit flavours like strawberry. It's very cold, and may come from China, but became very popular in Italy and the UK about three hundred years ago.

5 Write descriptions like the ones in Exercise 4 for a food or drink you know. Then work in pairs. Guess your partner's food.

This is a sweet and spicy dish. It comes from Peru. It has fish, onions, hot pepper and lime juice.

Ceviche?

Pad Thai is a popular dish from Thailand. It is made with noodles, prawns or chicken, eggs, garlic and chilli peppers.

LISTENING

6 Work in pairs. Look at the photo. Why do you think people want to grow vegetables under the sea?

7 Listen to a conversation. Which two of the topics (a–c) do the people talk about? Write 1 and 2 in the order you hear them. There is one extra topic. 🎧 **41**

a food for the future
b the importance of smell
c tasting what we see

8 Listen to the conversation again. Are the sentences true (T) or false (F)? 🎧 **41**

1 Mark gives Kasia something spicy to taste.
2 Kasia tastes more with her nose closed.
3 The nose is more important than the mouth for tasting.
4 When Kasia has a cold, the only thing she can taste is sweet food.
5 There will be a lot more people on Earth in about thirty years.
6 In the future, meat might come from laboratories instead of farms.
7 Scientists are already growing fruit under the sea.
8 More land will be necessary for farms in the future.

9 MY PERSPECTIVE

Work in pairs. Answer the questions.

1 Do you think it will be possible to grow food in laboratories or under the sea in the future?
2 Would you like to eat food from laboratories, or from under the sea? Why? / Why not?
3 What other ways are there of growing enough food for all the people on Earth? Can you think of any?

10 PRONUNCIATION Minimal pairs

> Sometimes, only one sound makes the difference between words, for example *paper* and *pepper*.

a Listen to the sentences. Which word do you hear? 🎧 **42**
   1 I need some *paper* / *pepper* for my project.
   2 Can I *taste* / *toast* this bread?
   3 I think green tea is *better* / *bitter*.
   4 I need more *spice* / *space* for my project.
   5 Did you smell the *soap* / *soup*?

b Work in pairs. Listen again. Then practise saying the sentences with both words. Can your partner tell which word you're saying? 🎧 **42**

Divers look after an underwater basil farm in Italy.

GRAMMAR Predictions and arrangements

11 Look at the examples in the Grammar box. Answer the questions.

Predictions and arrangements

Talking about future arrangements

a *I'm giving my presentation next Thursday.*

b *I'm going to try that with my brother sometime.*

Making predictions

c *There will be nearly ten billion people on Earth in 2050.*

d *We're going to need more food.*

e *I guess we won't need as much land for farms.*

f *We might 'grow' meat in laboratories.*

g *We might not have farm animals for food.*

1 What time period do all the sentences talk about: the present or the future?
2 Which sentence uses a present tense verb form?
3 Which sentence, a or b, describes a more certain or fixed arrangement?
4 What is the shortened form of *will not*?
5 Which is more certain: *will* or *might*?
6 For sentence d, do we know that more food will be necessary? How do we know?

Check your answers on page 140. Do Exercises 1–6.

12 Choose the correct options to complete the announcement.

Science Day: Feeding a growing population

The science department (1) *is holding / might hold* a discussion next Monday from 3:00 to 4:00 about the future of food, and all students are invited to attend. According to science teacher Mr Yamada, 'Scientists think there (2) *will be / are being* nearly ten billion people on Earth in 2050. As the population increases, we (3) *might not / will* need more food. We (4) *are going to / won't be able to* continue raising animals for food, because it uses a lot of energy.' According to Yamada, this is where the science gets interesting. 'To feed everyone in 2050, (5) *we might have to "grow" / we'll "grow"* meat in laboratories.' Yamada also says that scientists are working on new ways to grow food. 'Right now, researchers (6) *will experiment / are experimenting* with new ways of growing food, for example growing in tunnels under the ground,' he explains. 'In 2050, underground farmers (7) *won't have to / aren't having to* worry so much about the weather!'

13 Complete each sentence. Use one verb with *going to* and one verb in the present continuous.

1 My dad ____is buying____ (buy) a 3D food printer next week because he thinks food printing __is going to be__ (be) the next big thing.

2 We're _____ (have) dinner with our vegetarian friends next week, so I_____ (eat) vegetarian food this weekend to see what it's like.

3 Layla_____ (give) a presentation tomorrow about how future farmers_____ (grow) vegetables underwater.

4 I_____ (have) a big steak dinner tomorrow night, and I_____ (enjoy) it, because there won't be much real meat in the future!

14 Work in groups. Look at the list of special occasions. Pick one and plan activities and a way to celebrate. Compare your plans with another group.

birthday	end of a sports season	good grades
graduation	university acceptance	wedding

It's Marcos's birthday. We're going to have a party at the park on Saturday. We're going to eat at 1:00pm.

7B The greatest human success story

VOCABULARY BUILDING Suffixes

> Adding -er, -ment or -ance to some verbs creates nouns.
>
> • -er is added to mean 'a person who does something' (work → worker).\
>
> • -ment is added to mean 'the result of the verb' (enjoy → enjoyment).
>
> • -ance is added to mean 'a specific instance of the verb happening' (perform → performance).
>
> Note the spelling rules for -er suffixes.
>
> When a verb ends in a consonant, -er can be added (worker).
>
> When a verb ends in one vowel + b, d, f, l, m, n, p or t, the final letter is usually doubled (runner).
>
> When a verb ends in e, add -r (baker).

1 Read the Vocabulary building box. Then add a suffix to items 1–4 to make a noun. Use a dictionary if necessary.

People
1 travel -
2 work -

Other nouns
3 achieve -
4 disappear -

READING

2 Read the first two paragraphs of the article. Find three more nouns that are made from verbs.

3 Read about identifying the main theme of a paragraph. Then read the article and put letters for the the headings (a–f) next to the correct paragraph.

> Each paragraph of a text usually has a different main idea. By identifying the main idea of each paragraph, we can better understand the whole text. Usually, focusing on the nouns and verbs in a paragraph gives you a good idea of its main ideas.

  a Staying in one place
  b The most important workers on the farm
  c Once upon a time
  d Protecting our farms
  e Our greatest achievement?
  f A long history together

4 Read the article again. Underline the information that disagrees with each statement below.

1 The first farmers lived about five thousand years ago.
2 Plants can grow food on their own.
3 Working on farms stopped humans from making progress in other areas.
4 Bees sometimes cause problems because they eat plants.
5 Farmers dislike bees, so they try to kill them.

5 Match the farming vocabulary from the article (1–8) with the best definition (a–h).

1 agriculture
2 livestock
3 community
4 crop
5 grow
6 harvest
7 plant
8 season

  a animals raised for meat
  b a food plant
  c to collect food from plants
  d farming
  e part of the year
  f to put a plant into the ground
  g to give a plant what it needs to develop
  h a group of people who live or work together, or who have something in common

6 Do the following. Use a dictionary if necessary.

1 Name two types of livestock.
2 Names two crops that grow in your country.
3 Put these words in the order that farmers do them: harvest, plant, grow.
4 Name two or three places in your region or country where there are a lot of farms.

7 Work in pairs. Cover the article. Tell each other what you have learned about these things.

• how agriculture changed the lives of humans.
• why bees are important.
• a reason why bees may be disappearing.

8 CHOOSE

1 Read the labels on the photo. Discuss in pairs. What food have you eaten recently that would be gone if bees disappeared?

2 Read the labels on the photo. Write a shopping list for a dinner party. All dishes must use food that's pollenated by bees.

3 Use the internet to find more information about the decreasing bee population. Write a list of things that people can do to help.

> '*Almost all the fruits and nuts, and a lot of the vegetable varieties that we eat require some insect – usually bees – for pollination.*'

SAM DROEGE, BEE EXPERT

PB & J
No jelly or peanut butter

No salsa

No guacamole
(no avocados)

Pasta salad
Pasta is OK, but no broccoli, olives, onions, peppers or tomatoes

Blackberry pie
No berries

Greek salad
No tomatoes, cucumbers, onions or olives. Feta cheese is OK, but too salty without the vegetables!

Fruit salad
Banana and pineapple only. No strawberries, grapes, blueberries or kiwi.

Lemonade
No lemons, so it's just sugar and water. Too sweet!

Kebabs
Meat is OK, but no onions, peppers or tomatoes

The most important farmers

🎧 **43** _____ Before the first farms appeared, humans were hunters, following animals and the seasons from place to place. Along with the meat they killed, they ate fruit, vegetables and nuts that
5 they found as they travelled. And then, in different places all over the world, people began farming. This happened at least 10,000 years ago.

_____ One requirement of farming is that people stay in one place. Farmers need time to plant crops
10 in the spring, care for them through the summer and harvest them in the autumn. Livestock that is raised for meat needs to stay where there is a good supply of food and water.

_____ This required people to work together as
15 a community: some farmed, some tended to the livestock, some built houses or cooked. Farmers had to work hard to keep everyone fed, but none of this was possible without one creature: bees. These hardworking insects transfer pollen from plant to
20 plant. This causes healthy plants to produce fruit and vegetables, both on farms and in nature. Without bees, most plants can't make the things people eat – from apples to corn to tomatoes. Eventually, people began keeping bees in order to help with the crops as well as
25 provide honey.

_____ Experts believe that bees were domesticated 4,500 years ago in Egypt. This allowed for more crops, and bigger cities and towns to grow. As villages and towns grew, people built more and more houses
30 to live in and buildings to store food. Bees come in handy here, too. Experts think that containers made from beeswax started being used for storage at least 9,000 years ago.

_____ We've been to the moon, but agriculture
35 is probably the biggest human success story. You may not think about it often, but almost everything you eat every day is a product of farming. By growing our food rather than finding it or hunting for it, we have allowed ourselves to think new thoughts
40 and make new things. We have turned our villages into towns and our towns into great cities and created the modern world – all possible only because of bees.

_____ Recently, the number of bees has dropped. Why? Some insects eat plants, so farmers use chemicals
45 to kill these insects. But this also can kill bees. We now know that the disappearance of bees around the world is an increasing problem and these chemicals are one of the causes. If we keep losing bees, we may soon have difficulty growing food. Some experts believe that
50 if farmers continue using chemicals, the bee population will continue to fall. Fortunately, farmers are beginning to understand the situation and are finding safer ways to fight the insects that cause problems. Farming will continue to be our greatest success story only if we
55 protect the bees.

The countryside near Kars, Turkey

7C A taste of honey

GRAMMAR First conditional

❶ Look at the examples in the Grammar box and answer the questions.

> **First conditional**
>
> If we **protect** the bees, farming **will continue** to be our greatest success story.
>
> If we **keep** losing bees, we **may** soon **have** difficulty growing food.
>
> If farmers **continue** using chemicals, the bee population **will continue** to fall.
>
> Bees **will return** only when we **stop** using dangerous chemicals.

1 Which clause gives us the result of a possible action, the *if* clause or the other clause?
2 Are the actions in the result clauses possible or not?
3 What tense is used for the *if* or *when* clause?
4 What tense is used in the result clause?
5 Which is more certain, *if* or *when*?

Check your answers on page 140. Do Exercises 7–10.

❷ Put the phrases (a–d) in the best place to complete the text.

The Balyolu – Turkey's Honey Road
If you go walking in the countryside near the Turkish city of Kars, (1) ___d___ – or several. For centuries, the local people have raised bees for the honey they make. And you'll certainly have a chance to taste some if (2) _____ . If you taste carefully, (3) _____ as you move along the trail. But watch out! If (4) _____ , you could ruin your trip with a stomach ache!

a you walk the Honey Road
b you eat too much honey
c you may notice the changing flavours in the honey
-d- you might meet a beekeeper*

beekeeper *a person who takes care of bees and gathers their honey*

❸ Choose the best words to complete the article.

Saving food traditions for the future
The Honey Road was the idea of National Geographic Explorer Catherine Jaffee. Why is honey important to her? All over the world, young people are moving from rural areas to cities. If they (1) *leave / will leave* their villages, they (2) *didn't / won't* continue to learn about their own local food and food traditions – like beekeeping. She believes that if we (3) *don't / will* keep traditions like beekeeping alive, (4) *we / we may* lose them forever – and lose part of who we are. Thanks to efforts like this, (5) *will / when* future generations look back, (6) *they will / they* thank us for keeping foods and traditions alive.

4 Choose *if* or *when* to complete the exchanges.

1 A: Are you coming to Kars next month?
   B: Yes. *When* / *If* I get there, I'll call you.

2 A: It may rain tomorrow.
   B: *When* / *If* it rains, the bees won't be active.

3 A: We have one more hour to work on our project today.
   B: *When* / *If* we work quickly, we may finish it.

4 A: I have an appointment with Mr Sato tomorrow.
   B: *When* / *If* you see him, say hello for me.

5 A: I might go shopping this afternoon. I'd like to get some ice cream for this evening.
   B: Well, *if* / *when* you go, could you get some honey for me?

5 Listen to the exchanges and check your answers to Exercise 4. 🎧 **44**

6 Work in pairs. Write your own endings to the sentences. Use *will*, *may*, *could* and *might* at least once each.

1 If I get hungry before the end of school today, I …
2 When I have dinner tonight, I …
3 If my friends and I have lunch together next week, we …
4 When I get home from school today, I …
5 If we go to a restaurant for my next birthday, we …
6 If the weather's good at the weekend, …
7 When school finishes next month, …
8 If I get good marks in my end-of-year exams, …

7 Work in groups. Discuss what you have learned in this unit by making 'conditional chains'. Start with the following.

1 If we protect bees, …

protect bees ⟶ no pollen problem ⟶ plants grow well ⟶ plants make food ⟶ people have enough food for the future

A: *If we protect bees, there will be no pollen problem.*
B: *If there is no pollen problem, plants will grow well.*
C: *If plants grow well, they'll make food.*

2 If people leave rural areas to live in cities, …

not enough people to work ⟶ farms and factories close ⟶ villages start to die ⟶ more people leave ⟶ cities become overcrowded

3 If we grow vegetables underwater, …

8 CHOOSE

1 Work in pairs. Pick one of the issues in Exercise 7. Discuss what people can do at each part of the chain to help the situation.

2 Write a paragraph using one of the chains to guide you.

3 Work in groups. Think of a new issue and make a conditional chain. Present your ideas to the class.

A beekeeper in Turkey collects honey – one of the world's most ancient foods.

> # " The best thing to do with food is to eat and enjoy it, and to stop wasting it. "

TRISTRAM STUART

Read about Tristram Stuart and get ready to watch his TED Talk. ▶ **7.0**

AUTHENTIC LISTENING SKILLS

Prediction

Sometimes you can use what you already know about a topic to predict what a speaker might say. This can help you understand more of what you hear.

1 Read the Authentic listening skills box. Based on the title of the talk and the quote above, what do you think Tristram Stuart is likely to talk about? Tick (√) the topics you think he may discuss.

Hunger isn't a big problem in rich countries.

Cooking is a useful skill.

Fast food often isn't very tasty.

The biggest problem isn't too little food, but too much.

We need to stop wasting food.

We can save money by eating less.

2 Listen to an extract from the talk and check your answers to Exercise 1. 🎧 **45**

WATCH

3 Watch Part 1 of the talk. Choose the correct option to complete each sentence. ▶ **7.1**

1 People started trying to create a food surplus _____ years ago.
  a 1,200   **b** 12,000   **c** 120,000

2 Now, our agriculture cuts too many trees, uses too much _____ and pollutes the air.
  a space   **b** gas   **c** water

3 Tristram found some packets of biscuits in the rubbish behind a _____ .
  a supermarket   **b** restaurant   **c** house

4 Watch Part 2 of the talk. Write the correct numbers to complete the pie chart. ▶ **7.2**

Food use and waste

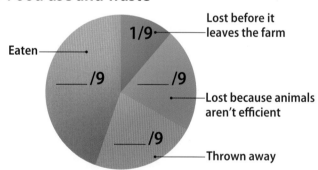

5 Watch Part 3 of the talk. Answer the questions. ▶ **7.3**

1 Tristram shows a picture of thrown away packaged food. Where was it thrown away?

2 How many slices of bread did the factory throw away each day?

3 The farmer had to throw away the spinach crop because something was growing with it. What was it?

TEDTALKS

6 Watch Part 4 of the talk. Choose the correct option to complete each sentence. ▶ 7.4

1 Tristram says we need to tell *friends and neighbours* / *corporations and governments* to stop food waste.
2 He says we should store lettuce in *the fridge* / *a vase of water*.
3 Tristram *fed 'waste' food to* / *collected 'waste' food from* 5,000 people.

7 **VOCABULARY IN CONTEXT**

a Watch the clips from the talk. Choose the correct meaning of the words or phrases. ▶ 7.5

b Complete the sentences with your own words. Discuss your answers with a partner.

1 _____ is a *global* challenge.
2 The people who live in my *household* are _____ .
3 The government should *invest* more money in _____ .
4 A *resource* I can help conserve (keep safe) is _____ .
5 A problem that needs to be *tackled* in my community is _____ .

CRITICAL THINKING Supporting evidence

When people present an idea, they often give examples to support their idea. This makes the idea more believable.

8 Match Tristram's ideas (1–4) with the examples that support them (a–d).

1 Supermarkets waste food.
2 The sandwich industry wastes bread.
3 Cosmetic standards cause food waste.
4 We can store food in a better way.

a a photo of discarded bread crusts
b photos of lettuce stored correctly and incorrectly
c a photo of packaged foods on a shelf
d photos of piles of wasted parsnips, oranges, and bananas

9 Work in pairs. Discuss the questions.

- Who do you think sets cosmetic standards for food?
- Are cosmetic standards for food important to you personally? Why? / Why not?
- Do you see food waste at your school? What could be done to reduce it?

CHALLENGE

Which of the ideas from Tristram's talk could you or would you try? Tell your partner and explain your reasons.

- eating sandwiches made with the ends of a loaf of bread
- eating safe, fresh food that the supermarket has thrown away
- eating fruits or vegetables that don't look perfect
- organizing campaigns to get companies or governments to reduce food waste
- organizing an event to celebrate food

7E What's it like?

All over the world, people love to eat together and share food with friends.

SPEAKING

1 Look at the photo. Answer the questions.

1 What different types of food can you see in the picture?
2 Where do you think this is? Have you ever eaten somewhere like this? Did you enjoy it? Why? / Why not?
3 What types of food would you choose for an informal party with your friends?

2 Look at the Useful language box. Then listen to the conversation. What are the people planning? Tick (√) the expressions you hear from the Useful language box. 🎧 46

3 Listen again. Choose the correct option to complete each sentence. 🎧 46

1 The people are going to have a *picnic / barbecue*.
2 Halloumi is a kind of *cheese / fish*.
3 Halloumi can be a little *sour / salty*.
4 The vegetarians who are coming can eat bread and *salad / fish*.
5 People can bring their own *food / drinks*.
6 They can get the knives and forks from the *school / supermarket*.

4 Imagine you're planning a meal for a party with your class. What food and drinks would you like to include? Make notes.

5 Work in small groups. Think about the meal you are planning. Use your notes from Exercise 4. Make suggestions of different food, and practise describing the different types. Use expressions from the Useful language box.

WRITING A restaurant review

6 Work in pairs. Answer the questions.

1 What kind of restaurants does your town or city have?
2 What is the most popular type of casual food in your area? Do you like this food?
3 What restaurant would you go to with a visitor to your town or city? Why?

7 Read the restaurant review on page 151. Answer the questions.

    1 Where is the restaurant?
    2 When is it open?
    3 What is the atmosphere like?
    4 What type of food does it have?
    5 Is it expensive?
    6 Does the writer recommend it?

8 **WRITING SKILL** Writing a review

A review usually contains all or some of the following information. Tick (√) the information below that is in the review.

- where something is
- when it is open/available
- what it is like
- good points about it
- bad points about it
- what is different about it
- whether the writer recommends it

9 Work in small groups. Think of two or three restaurants or eating areas. Discuss where they're located, when they're open, what the atmosphere is like, and what kind of food they have.

10 Choose one place from Exercise 9 and write a review of it. Use the model on page 151 to help you, and the expressions from the Useful language box. Include all of the points from Exercise 8.

11 Exchange reviews with a partner. Check each other's work. Does it answer the questions in Exercise 7?

Useful language

Describing a restaurant

It's in / at …
It's open on …, from … to …
It's a very (relaxing / unfriendly) place.
The service is (fast / friendly / slow).
The food is (simple / tasty / horrible).
One advantage / disadvantage of the restaurant is …
It costs about … to eat here.
I would definitely recommend … because …
I wouldn't recommend … because …

8 Buyer's choice

A woman shops for shoes at a mall in Hefei, China.

8A Why we buy

VOCABULARY A product's life

1 Work in pairs. Discuss the questions.

- What kind of things do you buy for yourself? Clothes? Music? Books? Other things?
- Where do you like to shop? Online? In stores? At markets or shopping malls? In department stores?
- Look at the photo. What would you do if you had this many options? How would you choose what to buy? What would be important to you (price, colour, style, etc.)?

2 Complete the sentences with the correct words.

advertises	design	grows	manufacture	material
pick	produce	~~recycle~~	sell	~~throw away~~

1 He will ___*recycle*___ the bottles, not ___*throw*___ them ___*away*___ .
2 The company _____ online and on TV.
3 The _____ is made from wool and cotton.
4 The artist created a good _____ for the new product.
5 Farmworkers _____ the fruit after it _____ .
6 Machines are used to _____ the goods. Machines can _____ faster than people can.
7 She is going to _____ her goods at the market.

3 Choose the correct option to complete the sentences about a clothing company.

Kuyichi …

1 *designs* / *throws away* really cool clothes.
2 pays a fair price for cotton from the farmers who *grow* / *manufacture* it.
3 also uses cotton *picked* / *recycled* from old clothes.
4 uses factories in Tunisia, Turkey, China, India and Macedonia to *sell* / *manufacture* the clothes.
5 *produces* / *advertises* with phrases such as 'pure goods'.
6 *sells* / *picks* their clothes through their online store.
7 asks customers not to *throw away* / *recycle* old clothes.
8 wants customers to *throw away* / *recycle* old clothes or give them to charity.

4 MY PERSPECTIVE

Look at the information in Exercise 3. Work in pairs. Discuss the questions.

- Kuyichi's advertisements say they are doing good in the world. Do you agree that they are? Why? / Why not?
- Does doing good things for the world, like recycling, help sell products?
- What advertisements have you seen recently? What did they say or show?
- Did the adverts you want to buy something? How did they try to persuade you?

5 How do the choices you make when shopping affect these things?

- your wallet
- the environment
- your self-esteem
- your community

LISTENING

6 Look at the infographic. Match the steps in the life of a shirt (1–6) with the labels (a–f).

  a design and produce the shirt *3*
  b advertise and sell it
  c grow and pick cotton
  d throw it away or recycle it
  e manufacture the cotton material
  f deliver the shirt to stores

7 Listen to a fashion podcast about Kuyichi clothes. Number the topics in the order Pietro and Agata talk about them. 🎧 47

  a cotton recycling
  b the design of the clothes
  c cotton growers
  d where you can buy them
  e producing Kuyichi clothes
  f reducing waste and pollution
  g advertisements
  h the topic of today's show *1*
  i recycling Kuyichi clothes

8 Listen to the podcast again. Choose the correct option to complete each sentence. 🎧 47

  1 Kuyichi is a company from *the Netherlands* / *Japan*.
  2 Some of their advertisements say, '*love fashion.*' / '*love the world.*'
  3 Some of their cotton growers are in *Turkey* / *Brazil*.
  4 They use recycled material to reduce *price* / *waste*.
  5 Pietro wears Kuyichi clothes because they *fit well* / *look good*.
  6 Kuyichi makes some of its clothes in *China* / *Thailand*.
  7 Pietro says that buying online is the *cheapest* / *easiest* way.
  8 Kuyichi *wants* / *doesn't want* their clothes to go to charity.

9 What 'good' things does Kuyichi do? Work in pairs. Make a list of the good things you can remember from the podcast. Would these make you more likely to shop at Kuyichi? Why? / Why not?

  They recycle cotton from old clothes. I think that's really good because it helps to reduce waste.

94 Unit 8 Buyer's choice

GRAMMAR Second conditional

10 Look at the sentences in the Grammar box. Choose the correct option to complete each sentence.

> ### Second conditional
>
> **a** *If more companies **were** like Kuyichi, the world **would be** a better place.*
>
> **b** *If they **didn't look** good, I **wouldn't wear** them.*
>
> **c** *If you **wanted** to buy some tomorrow, that **would** probably **be** the easiest way.*

1 There *are / aren't* a lot of companies like Kuyichi.
2 The world *is / isn't* a better place.
3 Kuyichi's clothes *look / don't look* good.
4 The speaker *wears / doesn't wear* Kuyichi clothes.
5 It is *quite / not very* likely that the presenter will buy some Kuyichi clothes tomorrow.
6 The *If* clause of sentences a and b talks about *the past / a situation that isn't real*.
7 The *if* clause of sentence c talks about something that isn't *likely / unlikely*.

Check your answers on page 142. Do Exercises 1–2.

11 Put the words in the correct order to make sentences.

1 sell anything / we wouldn't / If we / advertise, / didn't
2 your old clothes, / If you didn't / you could / throw away / recycle them
3 grow cotton / They would / didn't grow corn / if they
4 would sell / The store / if it were / more things / bigger
5 a coat, / you could / If / make it / I designed
6 online / sold them / We could / for less if / sell our products / we
7 more clothes / used / would buy / if / I / recycled materials / they
8 if they / would / Clothes / didn't have to / be / travel so far / cheaper

> ### First and second conditional
>
> **a** *If you **look** at their advertisements, you**'ll see** phrases like 'pure goods' and 'love the world'.*
>
> **b** *If you **wanted** to buy some tomorrow, that **would** probably **be** the easiest way.*

12 Look at the two sentences in the Grammar box. Answer the questions.

1 Which sentence is a first conditional? Which is a second conditional?
2 Which action in the *if* clause is more likely to happen, the one in sentence a or the one in sentence b?
3 Which tenses or verb forms do we use in the two conditionals?

Check your answers on page 142. Do Exercises 3–5.

13 Match the two parts of the sentences. Then say whether each sentence is first conditional or second conditional. If necessary, review the first conditional on page 140.

1 If companies pay workers well,
2 If companies don't advertise,
3 If billboards were beautiful,
4 If companies didn't advertise,
5 If customers like an advertisement,
6 If companies paid workers more,

a people won't know about their products.
b people wouldn't know about their products.
c people wouldn't want to remove them.
d they would work harder.
e they will buy a product.
f they will be happy.

14 Choose the correct options to complete the article about advertisements in cities.

The mayor of São Paulo, Brazil, wanted to make his city a better place, so he made a law banning billboards. He called outdoor advertisements a type of pollution. Other cities have now done the same thing. If you go to Chennai in India, (1) *you'll / you would* notice a difference from other big cities in India as a 2009 law ended outdoor advertising. And you won't see any billboards if you (2) *will walk / walk* down the streets of Grenoble, in France, either. Tehran, in Iran, replaced 1,500 billboards with art for ten days. The change was popular, and many people (3) *will / would* be happy if it happened again. But not every city is ready to stop advertising. If you (4) *took / take* the famous billboards away from New York's Times Square, you'd ruin one of the city's most famous tourist attractions. And would people visit Piccadilly Circus in London if its famous advertisements (5) *aren't / weren't* there?

15 Work in pairs. Discuss the questions. Take notes. Remember to use the second conditional.

- If you were able to change your town or city to make it a better place, how would you change it?
- If your town had no advertising, how would it be different?
- How would people in your town feel if advertising were stopped?

16 MY PERSPECTIVE

Work in small groups. Using the ideas you discussed in Exercise 15, prepare a presentation about why you think billboards should or shouldn't be allowed in your town or city.

8B Saving the surf

VOCABULARY BUILDING Compound nouns

> Compound nouns can be:
> - two words joined to make one word, like *billboard*
> - two words used together to name one thing, but not joined, like *tourist attraction*
>
> The first word always tells us something about the second. For example, a *billboard* is a type of *board*, not a type of *bill*.

1 Read the Vocabulary building box. Then match the words to make compound nouns.

1	shopping	**a**	pollution
2	air	**b**	forests
3	sea	**c**	bags
4	rain	**d**	programme
5	recycling	**e**	life

2 **PRONUNCIATION** Compound noun stress

Listen to the words. Notice the stress. Practise saying them with a partner. 🎧 **48**

3 Complete the sentences with the compound nouns from Exercise 1.

1 Many supermarkets make shoppers pay for _____ .
2 Plastic bags can end up in the ocean and hurt _____ .
3 Electric cars will help to reduce _____ .
4 In most countries, selling new wood products that come from _____ is not allowed.
5 The Body Shop was one of the first shops to have a _____ for customers to return empty bottles.

READING

4 Work in pairs. Look at the compound nouns from the article. What do you think they mean? What kind of company do you think the article is about?

fishermen   fishing boat   fishnet   skateboard   surfboard

5 Read the article. Choose the correct option to complete each sentence.

1 Kneppers and Stover enjoy *surfing / fishing*.
2 They were unhappy about *garbage / fishing boats* in the water.
3 Their company produces *fishnets / skateboards*.
4 They collect materials from *fishermen / the sea*.
5 Their customers *don't care / love* where the skateboards come from.
6 The first skateboards appeared in *Paris / Chile*.

6 Read the article again. Answer the questions.

1 What did Kneppers and Stover find in the ocean?
2 Who is Kevin Ahearn?
3 Where does the name of their company come from?
4 Why do fishermen throw their old nets into the sea?
5 In which countries can you find a Bureo board in a shop?

7 Read the information about pronouns. Then read the first paragraph of the article. Say what each pronoun refers to.

> In a text, pronouns such as *this*, *that*, *these*, *those*, *they*, *them*, *he*, *she* and *it* refer to other things in the text. For example, *I have a **new skateboard**. **It** was made in Chile.* Understanding these connections across sentences will help you understand the text.

1 Line 2: *they*
   a their surfboards   **b** Ben and David   **c** the waves
2 Line 6: *this*
   a surfing   **b** the waves   **c** finding trash
3 Line 8: *its*
   a the world   **b** action   **c** a friend
4 Line 16: *it*
   a Chile   **b** Bureo   **c** a skateboard

CRITICAL THINKING Identifying supporting information

> Writers can add specific information to make their text clearer and more interesting to read. Supporting information shows why certain facts are true or important.

8 Underline the supporting information in the sentences.

1 They often find lots of trash – plastic bags, bottles, and boxes – and old fishnets.
2 They started a business in Chile, one of their favourite surfing destinations.
3 They named their company Bureo, which means *the waves* in a native Chilean language.

9 Match the sentences in Exercise 8 with a reason (a–c) why the extra information was given.

a says why someone made a certain choice
b explains the meaning of an unfamiliar word
c gives specific examples of a more general word

Saving the surf

49 Ben Kneppers and Dave Stover love the ocean. And they love it most of all when they're on their surfboards. For them, there's nothing better than a day out on the waves. Unfortunately, when they go surfing,
5 they often find lots of trash* – plastic bags, bottles and boxes – and also old fishnets. And of course this makes them unhappy. But they know that if you just complain, the world won't change on its own, so they decided to take action. Ben
10 and Dave got together with a friend who also loves the ocean and surfing – Kevin Ahearn. They started a business in Chile, one of their favourite surfing destinations. They named their company
15 Bureo, which means *the waves* in a native Chilean language, and it designs, produces and sells skateboards.

What's the connection between skateboards and plastic garbage* in the
20 ocean? Fishnets are made of plastic. When workers on fishing boats need to throw away old or damaged nets, they usually just drop them into the sea.

It's easy to do, and there's no easy way to get rid of
25 them – until now. Bureo has set up a fishnet recycling programme that makes it easy to get rid of old nets. Instead of throwing them out of the boat and into the water, fishermen can leave their old nets at Bureo's recycling centres. This is almost as easy as throwing
30 them into the sea, and the local fishermen are happy to help clean up the ocean. Bureo has a factory in Chile which turns the old nets into plastic material to make skateboards. If Bureo wasn't doing
35 this work, tons of old fishnets would end up in the water as pollution. The company turns plastic garbage into something people want to buy.

Bureo sells its boards over the internet,
40 and also delivers them to shops in the US, Chile, Japan and Switzerland. Skaters everywhere love them not only because they're great skateboards, but also because they know that Bureo is
45 cleaning up the ocean, one old fishnet at a time.

WHO INVENTED SKATEBOARDS?

The first skateboards appeared in the 1940s, probably in Paris. A woman named Betty Magnuson reported seeing French children riding them in 1944, when she was working there. They made them by putting wheels on the bottom of old pieces of wood.

trash, garbage *rubbish (US English)*

One of Bureo's skateboards on top of the kind of fishnet it is made out of

8C New things from old ones

GRAMMAR Defining relative clauses

1 Read the extract in the Grammar box from the article about Bureo. In each sentence, what noun does the pronoun in bold refer to?

Defining relative clauses

*They got together with a friend **who** also loves the ocean and surfing – Kevin Ahearn. Bureo has set up a fishnet recycling programme **that** makes it easy to get rid of old nets. Bureo has a factory in Chile **which** turns the old nets into plastic material to make skateboards.*

2 Look at the extract in the Grammar box again. Choose the correct option to complete each sentence.

1 The pronouns *that*, *who* and *which* introduce more information about the nouns that come *before* / *after* them.
2 The pronoun *who* refers to *people* / *things* and the pronouns *that* and *which* usually refer to *people* / *things*.
3 The information that comes after the relative pronoun is *important* / *not important* to the meaning of the sentence.

3 Look at these two sentences. Can we leave out the pronoun when it is the subject or the object of the relative clause?

1 Bureo has set up a fishnet recycling programme that makes it easy to get rid of old nets.
2 Bureo has set up a fishnet recycling programme (that) many fishermen use.

Check your answers on page 142. Do Exercises 6–9.

4 Put the defining relative clauses in the correct places to complete the sentences.

1 Artijulos is an interesting home-furnishings shop ___*b*___ . These are things _____ – for example a vase _____ .

   a that used to be other things
   b that specializes in 'upcycled' products
   c that used to be a lightbulb

2 Asher Jay is a designer _____ . She brings attention to global issues _____ , including environmental and human-rights issues.

   a that need solutions
   b who creates art and advertising

3 Local First is an organization _____ to buy from businesses _____ in the same area where they're sold.

   a that make their products
   b that encourages consumers

4 Arthur Huang is an engineer _____ . When his company designed and built a store for Nike, he used materials _____ .

   a who believes in using recycled products
   b that were made from old bottles, cans and DVDs

French artist Paulo Grangeon makes pandas out of recycled paper. He shows the pandas at famous landmarks around the world.

5 Cross out the unnecessary relative pronouns in these sentences.

Recycling old clothes

1 What can you do with clothes which are too old or don't fit you any more?

2 If they're in good condition, why not give them to friends who might like them?

3 Put aside any clothes that you might wear again and look at them in a year.

4 Keep any in bright colours or with interesting patterns that you like and make them into other things, e.g. handbags or bed covers.

5 Give them to a charity which you like to help.

6 Put them in the recycling bins that the local government provides.

6 Complete each sentence with *who, that* or *which*, where necessary.

1 This is the shirt _____ I made.

2 Shopping isn't an activity _____ interests me.

3 I have a cousin _____ always gives me her old clothes.

4 This is the old leather jacket _____ I bought from my friend.

5 That's the shop _____ we like because the clothes aren't expensive.

6 She's the friend _____ went shopping with me last week.

7 Complete the article with relative pronouns where necessary.

Shopping for clothes to upcycle

Every year, about ten billion kilogrammes of old clothes and material (1) _____ no one wants end up in the rubbish. Erica Domesek, the fashion designer (2) _____ started the popular website psimadethis.com, wants to change that. She shows people (3) _____ want to dress in an original, interesting way how to upcycle old clothes. You can use your own old things (4) _____ you no longer wear, or cheap clothes (5) _____ come from thrift stores*. If you're someone (6) _____ loves shopping, the thrift store option is a good one. You get the pleasure (7) _____ comes from shopping without the pain of spending a lot of money. In one video, Erica shows how you can choose a T-shirt in a colour (8) _____ you really like, then turn it into a fashionable scarf.

thrift store *a shop that sells second-hand clothes*

8 Look at the list of words associated with shops and shopping. Use sentences with defining relative clauses to say what each thing is. Use a dictionary if necessary.

cash   checkout
clothes shop   credit card
customer   furniture shop
online shop   salesperson
second-hand shop   security guard
shopping centre   supermarket

A customer is a person who buys something in a shop.

9 CHOOSE

1 Use the internet to find photos of upcycled products. Write sentences that describe them. Use defining relative clauses. Share your ideas with the class.

2 Pick three places where you like to shop. Write definitions for each using relative clauses. See if a partner can guess each place.

3 Find out about another product like Bureo skateboards that comes from either recycled plastic or metal. Make a poster explaining how the recycling process works.

This table is upcycled from an old tractor.

" Go for it! Make that difference! "

MELATI AND ISABEL WIJSEN

Read about Melati and Isabel Wijsen and get ready to watch their TED Talk. ▶ **8.0**

AUTHENTIC LISTENING SKILLS

Content words

When you listen to authentic speech, you may not understand every word. However, the most important words – usually nouns and verbs – are often stressed. Listen for the stressed words and use them to figure out the meaning of what someone is saying.

1 Read the Authentic listening skills box. Then listen to part of the TED Talk. What do you notice about the underlined words? Practise saying the sentences with a partner. 🎧 **50**

In Bali, we generate <u>680 cubic metres</u> of <u>plastic garbage a day</u>. That's about a <u>fourteen-storey building</u>. And when it comes to <u>plastic bags</u>, less than <u>five percent</u> gets <u>recycled</u>.

2 Listen to another part of the talk. Complete it with the content words you hear. 🎧 **51**

We know that changes the image you may have of our
(1) _____ . It changed ours, too, when we learned about it, when we learned that almost (2) _____
plastic bags in (3) _____ end up in our drains and then in our (4) _____ and then in our
(5) _____ . And those that don't even make it to the ocean, they're either (6) _____ or littered.

WATCH

3 Work in pairs. Have you ever thought something going on at your school or home was wrong? Did you do anything about it? What did you do? Was anything else possible?

4 Watch Part 1 of the talk. Complete the notes. ▶ **8.1**

Two images of Bali: Island of gods and island of
(1) _____

Problem: most plastic bags aren't (2) _____ and end up in the ocean

Solution: say (3) _____ to plastic bags
Melati and Isabel: (4) _____ by Mahatma Gandhi to go on a (5) _____ strike

5 Watch Part 2 of the talk. Choose the correct option to complete each sentence. ▶ **8.2**

1 The governor of Bali agreed to *meet / talk on the phone with* the girls.
2 The governor *didn't promise / promised* to help them with their campaign.
3 Their campaign: for *shops and restaurants / beaches* to become 'bag-free' zones
4 They believe that *kids / only governments* have the power to change the world.
5 They want to stop people *in shops / at the airport* and ask about their plastic bags.

BYE BYE PLASTIC BAGS

6 VOCABULARY IN CONTEXT

a Watch the clips from the talk. Choose the correct meanings of the words and phrases. ▶ 8.3

b Complete the sentences so they are true for you.

1 Thinking of problems in the world, I'd like to *do something about* …
2 An example of a person who *walks his or her talk* is …
3 An example of a person who has *made a difference* in my life is …
4 A time in my life when I *went for it* was when I …
5 A person who is a good example for others and tries to *be the change* they want in the world is …

CRITICAL THINKING Understanding a speaker's authority

> When you think about a speaker's message, consider their experience. When a speaker talks about things they have actually done, their argument is stronger. They have more authority.

7 Isabel and Melati tell us to 'Go for it!' and to 'Make that difference.' What is the best reason why we should listen to them?

a They have watched other people successfully make changes in the world.
b They know that a lot of people believe that plastic bags are a serious problem.
c They've actually done what they're telling us to do, and they've succeeded.

CHALLENGE

Work in small groups. Isabel and Melati chose to make a positive change in their area. What could you and your friends do to make your world a better place? Think about the following:

- where you shop
- the things you buy
- how products are packaged
- what you do with things you no longer use

Take notes about your ideas.

8 Work in the same group. Plan a campaign like the one the Wijsen sisters started. Use your ideas from the Challenge box. Think about how you will start the campaign, what you will do, who will help you and how you will get more support. Present your ideas to the class.

8E Call to action

SPEAKING

1 Work in pairs. Answer the questions.

- Some shopping areas have pedestrian zones – areas that are closed to cars. Does your town or city have any pedestrian zones?
- What are the benefits of having shopping areas with no cars?
- What problems can be caused by closing roads?

2 Listen to the presentation. Choose the correct options to complete the paragraph. What is the speaker trying to persuade the audience to do? 🎧 52

We want to ban (1) *cars / people* from the high street. City centre (2) *entertainment / shopping* is an important part of the local economy. Research shows that people enjoy (3) *walking / eating* outdoors but don't like traffic or air pollution. A pleasant central area for (4) *families / teenagers* will mean a happier town. Allowing cars to ruin the (5) *shopping area / traffic* is wrong – people have a right to (6) *shop / feel safe.*

Speaking strategies

How to persuade

Use logic:
Research shows that …
Science has proven that …
If …, then …

Use emotion:
Think of …
How would you feel if …
My heart tells me that …

Use morals (right and wrong):
… is the right thing to do
It's wrong to …

3 Read the Speaking strategies box. Write the strategy that matches each quotation.

_____ Closing roads to traffic is the right thing to do. Allowing cars to spoil our shopping area is wrong.

_____ Think especially of families who have young children. They just want a nice place to go shopping.

_____ Research shows that people who shop downtown enjoy walking, but don't like the car and bus traffic.

4 Read the situations. In each case, how would you persuade people in your town to make a change? Brainstorm ideas as a class.

- People throw away a lot of metal, paper and plastic instead of recycling it.
- The city wants to build a shopping centre, but people think it will hurt local shops.
- A lot of old clothes end up in the rubbish. There should be a good way to exchange, re-use and upcycle clothes.

5 Work in small groups. Choose an idea from Exercise 4. Make a presentation persuading your audience to make a change. Use each of the three strategies in the box.

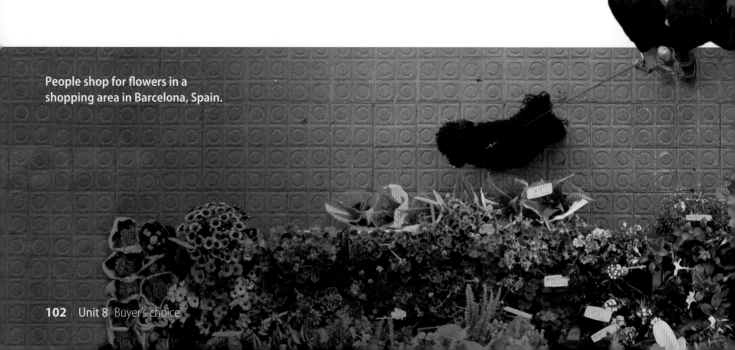

People shop for flowers in a shopping area in Barcelona, Spain.

WRITING A persuasive blog post

6 Work in pairs. Answer the questions.

- Do you have performers in the shopping areas of your town or city? What kinds?
- Do you think busking* should be allowed in busy shopping areas? Why?

busking *performing music in public places for money*

7 Read the blog post on page 152. Answer the questions.

1 What did the blogger love about Paris?
2 How does the blogger want to change their town's shopping area?
3 How does the blogger use logic?
4 How does the blogger use emotion?
5 How does the blogger use ideas of right and wrong?
6 Does the blog persuade you? Why?

8 **WRITING SKILL** Using persuasive language

a Read the Writing strategies box. Match the sentences (1–5) with points from the box (a–e).

1 Have you ever visited one? How did it make you feel?
2 When I was last in our capital city, I noticed …
3 I'd like you all to write a letter to ask …
4 It works really well there, and it's very popular.
5 It seems to me that it would be better for everyone if …

b Work in groups. What three new things would you like your area to have? Why?

We should have an art gallery. If we had one, then …

c Think of three possible arguments for each thing you chose in Exercise 8b, one logical, one emotional and one moral.

9 Choose one of your ideas from Exercise 8 and write a blog about it. Use the structure from the Writing strategies box.

10 Exchange blogs with a partner. Check each other's work. Does it use the ideas from the Writing strategies box? Does it persuade you about their ideas?

Writing strategies

Persuading people to make a change

a Introduce your topic with a personal story.
b Mention successful examples of the change you're arguing for.
c Ask readers to think of their own experience and describe the emotional side of your proposal.
d Explain what's wrong and what would be right.
e End with a call to action that explains exactly what you think people should do.

9 All in a day's work

Two women make fishing nets at the fishing village of Vinh Hy, Vietnam.

9A Work should be fun!

VOCABULARY Jobs

1 MY PERSPECTIVE

Work in pairs. Discuss the questions.

- Look at the photo. Would you like to have this job? Why? / Why not?
- Rank the aspects of a job from 1 (most important) to 5 (least important).

making a lot of money	working close to home
doing something you enjoy	being part of a team
doing something important with your life	

- Do you agree with the title of the lesson? Why? / Why not?

2 Match the jobs (1–10) with the correct description (a–j). Use a dictionary if necessary.

1	software developer	**a**	designs devices like smartphones
2	electronic engineer	**b**	gives people legal advice
3	nurse	**c**	helps people who are ill, usually with less training than a doctor
4	doctor		
5	accountant	**d**	designs computer programmes
6	secondary school teacher	**e**	helps teenagers learn
7	chef	**f**	prepares and inspects financial information and money
8	architect		
9	dentist	**g**	designs buildings
10	lawyer	**h**	provides care for people's teeth
		i	prepares and cooks food
		j	helps people who are ill, usually with more training than a nurse

3 Which workers are the most necessary? Rank the jobs from Exercise 2 from most to least needed in your country. (1 = most necessary, 10 = least necessary) Then look at page 154 to see which jobs are most needed worldwide.

4 Look at these jobs. Which category (1–5) does each one belong to? Think of one more job for each category. Use a dictionary if necessary.

chief executive	cleaner	construction worker	factory worker
firefighter	manager	office worker	paramedic
police officer	reporter	salesperson	shop manager

1 emergency services jobs
2 office or desk jobs
3 trades
4 retail jobs
5 other

5 Work in pairs. Answer the questions. Use these expressions.

- Which of the jobs in Exercises 2 and 4 would you most and least like to do?
- Are there other jobs not mentioned that you're interested in? What are they?

I'd like to be a(n) … because it's a(n) interesting / exciting / fun / well-paid job.

I wouldn't like to be a(n) … because it's a dangerous / boring / difficult / low-paid job.

LISTENING

6 Listen to Tomas and Julia talking about photographer Anand Varma. What's important to Julia in a job? What's important to Tomas? Write J or T. 🎧 53

adventure	fun	money
safety	staying near family	

7 Listen again. Are the sentences true (T) or false (F), or is the information not given (NG)? 🎧 53

1 Julia would like to travel for work.
2 Tomas has travelled a lot.
3 Julia hasn't decided exactly what job she wants yet.
4 Tomas says if Julia wants to have a job like Anand Varma, she can do it.
5 Tomas would like to have a job like Anand Varma's.
6 Tomas says he'd like to be a doctor.
7 For Julia, it's important to have an interesting job.
8 Julia thinks Tomas should consider being a paramedic.
9 Julia wants to make a lot of money.
10 Tomas wants a job that's very exciting.

8 MY PERSPECTIVE

Think of a job you liked in Exercise 5. What qualities or skills would you need for that job? Choose from the list or think of your own ideas.

be brave	be a hard worker
be organized	be strong
be good at cooking	be a good communicator

GRAMMAR Past perfect

9 Look at the words in bold in the Grammar box. How do we form the past perfect tense?

> **Past perfect**
>
> **a** *By the time he was a teenager, he**'d decided** he wanted to be a scientist.*
>
> **b** *He**'d** already **had** a job working in a fish shop before he started university.*
>
> **c** *He **hadn't worked** as a photographer before he got a job as an assistant photographer.*

Anand Varma is a science photographer and National Geographic explorer. In this photograph, he's at work in California, in the US.

10 Look at the examples in the Grammar box again. Choose the correct option to complete each sentence.

1 According to **a**, Anand decided to become a scientist *before / when* he was a teenager.

2 According to **b**, Anand worked in a fish shop *before / after* he went to university.

3 According to **c**, Anand *had / didn't have* experience working as a photographer before he became an assistant photographer.

4 We use the past perfect for actions in the past that happen *before / after* a more recent action.

11 Which two verb tenses are used in each sentence?

Check your answers on page 144. Do Exercises 1–4.

12 Write 1 or 2 in the brackets after each verb to show which action happened first and which happened second.

1 By the time my brother got (*2*) his first job, he had spent (*1*) a year working as a builder.

2 I had decided (__) to study electronic engineering, years before I left (__) school.

3 I went (__) to the interview, even though I had already accepted (__) another job.

4 My mother had trained (__) as a teacher before she had (__) the children.

5 By the time the company advertised (__) the job on its website, they had already chosen (__) the new sales manager.

13 Look at the timeline of Jacques-Yves Cousteau's life. Then use the words and time expressions to make sentences with the past simple and past perfect.

1 be 21 / discover love of the ocean (by the time)

By the time he was 21, he had discovered his love of the ocean.

2 Cousteau be in the navy for two years / travel around the world (when)

3 Cousteau give 20 years of his life to the ocean / receive money from the National Geographic Society for his work (when)

4 Cousteau write the book / *The Silent World* / make the film (before)

5 Cousteau be a TV star / for more than 15 years / he receive the Medal of Freedom (before)

6 he die / share his love of the ocean / with millions of people around the world (by the time)

14 Make a timeline of your life. Include at least five experiences or things you have learned, for example when you began studying English, when you started playing a sport or musical instrument, when you discovered something you love.

15 Work in pairs. Make sentences with the past simple and past perfect to describe each other's timelines.

By the time you were eight years old, you had discovered that you loved art.

When you were three, you had already started playing football.

16 Work in pairs. With your partner, discuss one or two jobs that would fit each other's life experiences and interests.

You've played football since you were three. Maybe you could be a professional footballer or a coach.

TIMELINE OF JACQUES-YVES COUSTEAU'S LIFE

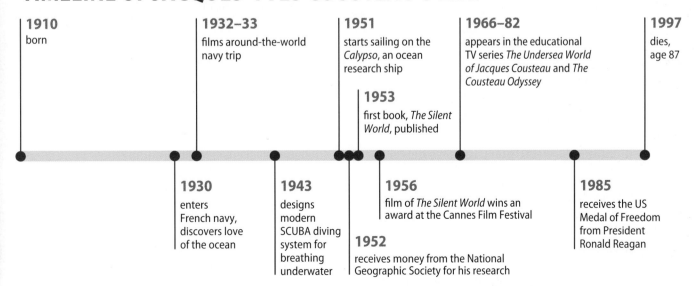

1910 born

1930 enters French navy, discovers love of the ocean

1932–33 films around-the-world navy trip

1943 designs modern SCUBA diving system for breathing underwater

1951 starts sailing on the *Calypso*, an ocean research ship

1952 receives money from the National Geographic Society for his research

1953 first book, *The Silent World*, published

1956 film of *The Silent World* wins an award at the Cannes Film Festival

1966–82 appears in the educational TV series *The Undersea World of Jacques Cousteau* and *The Cousteau Odyssey*

1985 receives the US Medal of Freedom from President Ronald Reagan

1997 dies, age 87

9B What do you want to be when you grow up?

VOCABULARY BUILDING Dependent prepositions

> Certain verbs are usually followed by a particular preposition. These dependent prepositions are followed by a noun or pronoun.
>
> We **asked for** help.
>
> Sometimes an object can go between the verb and preposition.
>
> I **borrowed** a pen **from** him.

1 Read the Vocabulary building box. Complete the sentences with the correct dependent preposition.

for	from	on	on	to	with

1 He applied _____ a job in a bank.
2 I agree _____ the idea of leaving school early if you want to start working.
3 They graduated _____ university last year and found work immediately.
4 How much money you earn depends _____ how many hours you work.
5 She introduced me _____ her brother.
6 You don't have to decide _____ a career in secondary school, or even in college or university.

READING

2 MY PERSPECTIVE

Do you agree or disagree with this statement? Why?

The main reason for going to school is to get a job.

3 Read about understanding different points of view. Then read the title of the survey. What are the three possible answers to the question in the title?

> Texts sometimes contain different points of view on a single topic. Understanding the different points of view can help you form your own opinion about the topic.

4 Read the survey. Which two writers …

1 answer *No?*   2 answer *Yes?*   3 answer *Maybe?*

5 Read the survey again. Choose the correct option to complete each sentence.

1 Lydia says that most of her school subjects were *useful / useless* for her job.
2 Sophia thinks school developed her *mind / study skills*.
3 Daniela learned skills for her job *at / after she left* school.
4 Paul believes that school sports develop *job skills / the body, but not the mind.*

5 Danh says that you study a lot of subjects to *prepare you for any possible career / discover what's interesting.*
6 Aslan says that paramedics and firefighters *don't learn their jobs at / don't usually finish* school.

6 Read the sentences. Who said each one?

1 History helped me develop critical thinking skills.
2 History is interesting, but not useful for my job.
3 The most important thing you learn about in school is yourself.
4 I don't remember what I learned in school.
5 School teaches you basic skills before you learn special skills for your job.

CRITICAL THINKING Identifying tone

> A writer's style of writing may affect how you feel about the subject. A pleasant or 'warm' tone can make you like the writer. A negative or 'cold' tone may make you want to disagree with them. A factual tone may consider more than one point of view and convince you to agree with the writer.

7 Read the Critical thinking box. Then answer the questions.

1 Which of the writers has a negative tone? How can you tell?
2 Which of the writers has the warmest tone? Why?
3 Which writers have a factual tone? How do you know?
4 Which answer do you agree with the most?

8 Read the responses. Whose *No* answer is each one addressing?

1 I can see what you're saying, but the jobs you mention involve a lot of skills, not just one. In those jobs – and in your job – you need to be able to look carefully at situations and to solve problems, sometimes very quickly. Those are skills you practise in school.
2 I see what you mean. You learn facts at school, but that isn't the main reason for going. When you do schoolwork, you develop study and research skills, and you also learn to work with people in an organization.

9 MY PERSPECTIVE

Work in groups. Discuss the questions.

- Think about the things you do at school. How do you think they prepare you for working life?
- Which school subjects do you think will be the most and least important for your future work?

Does school prepare you for the world of work?

54 **An online survey* asked working people around the world if school had prepared them for their jobs. Here's what six of those people said.**

If you want to be a software designer and build an
5 app, you don't need to know about history, literature
or biology. When I applied for my first job, I hadn't
learned any computer programming or project
management skills. Learning facts about Ancient Rome
and Ancient China was interesting, but I haven't used
10 them in my job. **– Lydia, software engineer**

My grandmother once told me that at school she hadn't
learned *what* to think; she'd learned *how* to think. I
agree with her. When we study history, we learn about
people, politics, mistakes in the past and the history of
15 great ideas. All of these things help us to understand
our place in the world and to learn to think clearly. By
the time I graduated from high school, I had definitely
learned to think. My grandmother was right! **– Sophia,
lawyer**

20 It depends on the type of job you want. If you want
to be a teacher, then school is the perfect preparation.
If you want to be a chef, school is a great start, but
then you need something more – you need to learn

all about food. When I got my first job, my boss said it
25 was the beginning of my education. **– Daniela, chef**

When you play football at school, you learn about the
sport – the rules, how to move the ball, etc. – but
you also learn about working with a team. In most
jobs, you work with some kind of team. Playing
30 sports at school definitely provided me with a lot of
teamwork skills. **– Paul, manager**

Most people don't become biologists, so studying
biology may not be useful for your job, so in some
cases, school doesn't prepare you very well. However,
35 school introduces you to a lot of ideas and subjects.
You probably need to study biology to discover if you
are interested in it or not. School helps you learn what
you like and don't like, and then you can decide on
the right career. Until my math teacher told me I could
40 become an accountant, I didn't know that job existed.
– Danh, accountant

Not at all – or at least not for me. Does a paramedic
learn to drive an ambulance at school? I don't think so.
Does a firefighter learn to fight fires at school? Never.
45 Sadly, for most jobs, you don't need to know the
things you learn in school. I forgot about school when
I started working. **– Aslan, construction worker**

*Comments adapted from Debate.org.

Spanish race car driver Carmen Jorda gets ready for another day at work.

'I entered my first go-kart race at the age of 12, but of course I was still going to school then, and I continued with my studies and university until I was 19. I started driving full time at age 20.'

9C She said it wasn't just about the money

GRAMMAR Reported speech

1 Look at the photo and quote. When does Carmen say she started racing? When does she say driving became her job?

Direct speech	Reported speech
Sophia's grandmother: 'At school, I **didn't learn** what to think; I **learned** how to think.'	*My grandmother once told me that at school she **hadn't learned** what to think; she**'d learned** how to think.*
The boss: 'This job **is** the beginning of your education.'	*When I got my first job, my boss said it **was** the beginning of my education.*
The maths teacher: 'You **can** become an accountant.'	*My maths teacher told me I **could** become an accountant.*
Lydia: 'I **haven't used** facts about Ancient Rome and Ancient China in my job.'	*Lydia said she **hadn't used** facts about Ancient Rome and Ancient China in her job.*

2 Look at the examples of direct speech and reported speech in the Grammar box. Then answer the questions.

1 What happens to the present simple in direct speech when we report the words?
2 What happens to the past simple?
3 What happens to the present perfect?
4 What happens to the modal verb *can*?
5 How do the pronouns *I* and *you* change?

Check your answers on page 144. Do Exercises 5–7.

3 Look at these words from Carmen's quote. Put them into reported speech.

1 I entered my first go-kart race at the age of 12 …
2 I continued with my studies and university …
3 I started driving full time at age 20.

4 Read Carmen Jorda's direct speech about her work. Complete the reported speech.

1 *My father took me to see my first Formula 1 Grand Prix at the age of eight.*
   Carmen said her father _____ her to see her first Formula 1 Grand Prix at the age of eight.
2 *At eleven I received my first go-kart.*
   She said she _____ her first go-kart when she was eleven.
3 *I've been working hard for a long time to get this opportunity.*
   She said she _____ working hard for a long time to get that opportunity.
4 *It has always been my dream. I train six days a week.*
   She said it _____ always been _____ dream and that she _____ six days a week.
5 *If one woman can do it, then many can achieve it!*
   She said if one woman _____ do it, then many _____ achieve it.

5 Listen to part of an interview with a teenage footballer who hopes to become a professional. Complete the interviewer's questions. 🎧 **55**

1 _____ becoming a professional footballer?
2 _____ enjoy the most about the game?
3 _____ played it?
4 _____ to football?
5 _____ to college or university?
6 Do you think _____ a scholarship*?

scholarship *money to pay for education for students who show special talent*

6 In your notebook, write Elena's answers to the questions from Exercise 5 as reported speech. You don't need to remember her exact words.

Elena said she was. She said there were probably more opportunities for boys, but that girls could be professional too.

7 Work in pairs. Take turns to ask and answer questions about the interview with Elena.

A: *He asked 'Are you thinking about becoming a professional footballer?'*

B: *She said she was …*

8 Work in groups of three, A, B and C. Take turns to start.

Student A: Think of something you did last weekend or have done today. Say it very quietly to Student B.
Student B: Report Student A's words quietly to Student C.
Student C: Tell Student A what he/she said.

A (to B): *I saw a great film at the weekend.*

B (to C): *Marco said he had seen a great film at the weekend.*

C (to A): *You saw a great film at the weekend.*

9 CHOOSE

- Work in pairs. Write down five questions to ask each other about school or after-school activities. Ask and answer the questions. Then use reported speech to explain your partner's answers to another pair.

- Find an interview with an athlete or another celebrity that you admire. Write about what they said using reported speech.

- Ask some adults you know for advice about preparing for the world of work. Give a short presentation explaining their answers. Use reported speech.

Two US high school students fight for the ball during a game of football. For some students, sports are a way to get into college.

> " When you're a child, anything and everything is possible. The challenge, so often, is hanging on to that as we grow up. "

DAME ELLEN MACARTHUR

Read about Dame Ellen MacArthur and get ready to watch her TED Talk. ▶ **9.0**

AUTHENTIC LISTENING SKILLS

Weak forms

Words such as prepositions (*to, of, from*), auxiliary verbs (*are, was*), conjunctions (*and, but*) and articles (*a, the*) aren't usually stressed. These unstressed words are called weak forms. The vowel sound in a weak form is usually the schwa sound, /ə/.

1 Read the Authentic listening skills box. Listen to the sentences from the talk. Underline two weak forms in the first sentence and three weak forms in the second. 🎧 **56**

1 When you're a child, anything and everything is possible.
2 The challenge, so often, is hanging on to that as we grow up.

2 Work in pairs. Underline the words that could be weak forms. Then listen and check. 🎧 **57**

1 I will never forget the excitement as we closed the coast.
2 I will never forget the feeling of adventure as I climbed on board the boat and stared into her tiny cabin for the first time.

WATCH

3 Watch Part 1 of the talk. Choose the correct responses for each question. ▶ **9.1**

1 Which three of these did Ellen experience when she first went on a boat?
  a challenge   **c** excitement   **e** danger
  b adventure   **d** freedom   **f** relaxation

2 Which two of these things did Ellen do to reach her goal of becoming a sailor?
  a saved to buy a boat   **c** worked in a boat shop
  b read books about sailing **d** took sailing classes

3 Ellen's school said that she wasn't clever enough to do what?
  a be a vet   **b** be a sailor   **c** go to college

4 When she was 21, Ellen met someone who helped her do which two things?
  a learn how to sail   **c** get a job in a company
  b design a boat   **d** sail around the world

4 Complete the experiences Ellen had when she sailed around the world. Then watch Part 2 of the talk and number them in the order she talks about them. ▶ **9.2**

blown   broke   ~~climbed~~   finished   hit   saw   took

a *climbed* to the top of the mast (the highest part of the sailing boat)
b _____ sunsets and wildlife
c almost _____ an iceberg   *1*
d were _____ over by the wind
e _____ everything she needed for three months
f _____ a speed record
g _____ in second position

5 Ellen says the race was both tough and amazing. Which experiences in Exercise 4 do you think were mostly tough? Which were mostly amazing?

6 Watch Part 3 of the talk. Correct the sentences. ▶ 9.3

1 Ellen realized suddenly that the global economy is ~~different from~~ living on a boat *the same as*.
2 She decided to continue the job of sailing around the world.
3 She talked to chief executives, experts, scientists and economists to teach them.
4 Her great-grandfather owned a coal mine.
5 According to the World Coal Association, there is enough coal for 180 more years.
6 Other valuable materials – copper, tin, zinc, silver – are not limited.

7 Watch Part 4 of the talk. Are these sentences true (T) or false (F), or is the information not give (NG)? ▶ 9.4

1 Ellen thinks we can stop waste in food packaging, car engines, electronic equipment and food.
2 Ellen thinks we should use energy efficient light bulbs.
3 When Ellen's great-grandfather was born, there were 25 cars in the world.
4 Ellen's great-grandfather designed the first computer.
5 Ellen says that her talk gives a plan for the future.
6 Ellen thinks young people should lead the change.

8 MY PERSPECTIVE

In the quote at the top of the page, Ellen says that anything is possible for children, and that the challenge is hanging on to that as we grow up. When you were very young, what did you think it would be like to be older? Is your perspective different now? How?

9 VOCABULARY IN CONTEXT

a Watch the clips from the talk. Choose the correct meaning of the words. ▶ 9.5

b Complete the sentences.
1 When I'm older, I'll have the *freedom* to …
2 My *toughest* class is …
3 If I go to college, I might *focus on* …
4 The *global* topic that I'm most interested in is …
5 I had … but I *used* it/them *up*.

10 Work in pairs. Discuss the questions.

• Ellen says her first trip was tough and amazing. What tough things have you done? What amazing things have you seen?
• Ellen's dream job was to be a sailor. Think about your dream job. How could you use it to make the world a better place?
• Have you had a moment when you 'connected the dots' and started to think differently about something? What?

CHALLENGE
Listen to another extract from Ellen's talk. Answer the questions. 🎧 58

1 When Ellen learned more about the world's finite materials, what did she do?
2 What did she realize about the world's economy?
3 Ellen ends the talk by saying *Now we have a plan*. What is Ellen's plan?

9E What does a UX designer do?

SPEAKING

1 Work in pairs. Look at the photo and discuss the questions.

- Does this workplace look interesting or boring to you? Why?
- Would you like to work like this? Why? / Why not?

2 Listen to part of a conversation between a student and a careers adviser. Choose the best words to complete each sentence. 🎧 **59**

1 The student *enjoys / doesn't enjoy* using computers.
2 A UX designer helps make products that are *beautiful to look at / easy to use*.
3 A lot of UX designers work for *schools / banks*.
4 If you want to be a UX designer, you should study *art / science*.

3 Listen again. Tick (√) the phrases in the Useful language box that you hear. 🎧 **59**

4 **PRONUNCIATION** Question intonation

a Listen again to the questions from the conversation. Notice how the intonation rises or falls at the end of the question. Mark it at the end of each question. 🎧 **60**

1 Have you ever heard of the job of UX designer? ⟶
2 Is it a computing job?
3 What does a user experience designer do?
4 Where do UX designers work?
5 Are UX designers well paid?

b Listen again. Practise saying the questions. 🎧 **60**

5 Work in pairs. Turn to page 154. Take turns asking and answering questions about jobs.

Turn to page 154.

Useful language

Talking about skills and interests

I love (computer games).
I get good marks in (IT). I like it.
I'm not very good at (languages).
I've always been interested in (software).
(Art) is one of my favourite subjects.
I'd like to work (with my hands / outside).

Asking about careers

What does a (UX designer) do?
Where do (UX designers) work?
What skills do (UX designers) need?
How much training does a (UX designer) have to take?
Are (UX designers) well paid?
How much do (UX designers) earn?
Where / How can I find out more about the job?

In many workplaces, people work together instead of having their own offices.

WRITING A formal email

6 Read the email on page 152. Tick (√) the information that the writer includes. Number the ones you have ticked in the order they appear.

the reason for writing
information about the reader's company
some information about the writer
a question about how much Mr Danoff earns
questions about how to learn more about UX design
a request for a reply

7 **WRITING SKILL** Indirect questions

a Read the Writing strategies box. Then read the email again. Underline how Ignacio asks the questions below in the email. Does he use direct or indirect questions?
   1 What are the most useful subjects?
   2 Do I need a university degree to work in UX design?
   3 Is there a website or magazine?

b Choose a job from Exercise 5. Write three direct questions about the job.

c Now rewrite the direct questions from Exercise 7b as indirect questions.
   1 Could you tell me _____ ?
   2 Do you know if _____ ?
   3 I'd like to know if _____ .

> **Writing strategies**
>
> Indirect questions are more polite than direct questions.
> Direct question: *What do you like about your job?*
> Indirect question: *Could you tell me what you like about your job?* / *I'd like to know what you enjoy about your job.*

8 Write an email to introduce yourself and ask for information about the job. Use the email on page 152 as a model.

9 Exchange emails with a partner. Check each other's work. Does it include the necessary information and use indirect questions?

10 Remote control

116

IN THIS UNIT YOU

- learn about how technology helps us explore the world around us – and ourselves

- hear about the history of communication technology

- read about how artificial intelligence is changing how we think about technology

- watch a TED Talk about how to control someone else's arm with your brain

- express and support opinions

Robots are starting to do
many jobs that people do.

10A Inventions: past, present, future

VOCABULARY Technology

1 Work in pairs. Answer the questions.

[handwritten: It's a robot operating a lawn mower. 2) Robots are cheaper + faster. Some people will lose their jobs.]

1 Look at the photo. What things can you see? Do you see any technologies that you recognize? What else do you think a robot like this could do?
2 Do you think this could really happen? What advantages or disadvantages are there in robots taking jobs from people?

2 Throughout history, technology has changed how people understand and connect to the world. Read the facts about technology. Match the words in bold (1–12) with the best category (a–g).

- When we think of (1) **technology**, we usually picture modern (2) **inventions** and (3) **digital** machines like smartphones, laptops and tablets. But technology is anything we make or use that helps us do something or (4) **control** the world we live in. Even simple office (5) **equipment** like pens, pencils and erasers were once important new (6) **developments**.
- Scientists used to believe that only humans made and used (7) **tools**, but in the 1960s, researcher Jane Goodall watched chimps go through a careful (8) **process** of taking leaves off small branches so they could use them to catch insects.
- (9) **Research** shows that nowadays many people feel that (10) **progress** in technology is too fast. They say we need to think more carefully about the possible drawbacks, such as what happens when our complicated (11) **electronic** equipment goes wrong. We can't usually just (12) **switch** the machine **off** and then switch it back **on** again!

a four nouns for things people use *[handwritten: 1, technology, inventions, equipment, tools]*
b two nouns that mean *change* or *improvement* *[handwritten: devts / progress]*
c one noun that means *a series of actions or steps to do something* *[handwritten: process 8]*
d one verb that means *to make someone or something do what you want* *[handwritten: control 4]*
e one noun that means *a careful study of something* *[handwritten: research 9]*
f two adjectives we often use when we talk about technology *[handwritten: digital 3 electronic 11]*
g one phrasal verb with two particles that means *start/stop something* *[handwritten: switch off/on 12]*

3 Complete the sentences using words from Exercise 2. Then discuss the question from item 1 with a partner.

1 Do we simply use our ___*technology*___ , or does it ___*control*___ us? Sometimes in this ___*digital*___ age, it can be difficult to know!
2 Recent ___*developments*___ have made computer ___*equipment*___ smaller and smaller.
3 People rely more and more on new ___*inventions*___ . But is this really ___*progress*___ ?
4 ___*Research*___ has found that these things aren't just ___*tools*___ that we use when we need them – many of us pay more attention to our smartphone than to the people around us.
5 Trying to teach yourself not to look at your phone so often can be a difficult ___*process*___ .
6 You should always ___*switch off*___ your computer properly so that you don't lose any work. We need to be careful with ___*electronic*___ equipment.

LISTENING

4 MY PERSPECTIVE

Which of these technologies are most useful for you? Rank them from 1 (most useful) to 6 (least useful). Then compare your list with a partner.

camera   computer   phone   printer   tablet   TV

5 Work in pairs. Discuss the questions.

- Do you use an electronic device every day? If so, what?
- What kind of problems can using electronic devices cause?
- How many different ways of communicating can you think of?
- Which way of communicating do you use most often? Why?

6 Look at the timeline about the history of communication technology at the bottom of the page. Match each type of communication below with a date on the timeline.

telephone

cell phone*

next big thing

smoke

bird

smartphone

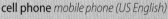
cell phone *mobile phone (US English)*

text message

7 Listen to the lecture and check your answers. 🎧 61

8 Listen again. Answer the questions. 🎧 61

1 What message was often sent by smoke signal?
2 Who used birds for communication?
3 Who probably had the first mail service?
4 Where did scientists develop the telegraph?
5 What was the message of the first phone call?
6 Why wasn't the mobile phone useful until 1979?
7 When did email become popular?
8 What was the first text message?
9 What does the speaker compare new technology to?

9 Work in pairs. What do *you* think could be the next big thing in communication technology?

GRAMMAR The passive

10 Look at the sentences from the lecture in the Grammar box. Underline the verb in each sentence. Circle the subject of each verb.

> **The passive**
>
> *Communication all over the world is seen as perfectly normal today.*
>
> *The first smoke message was sent about 10,000 years ago.*
>
> *The first telephone … was made in 1876.*
>
> *The first text message was sent in 1992.*

11 Read the sentences in the Grammar box again. Choose the correct option to complete each rule.

1 We form the passive with the verb *to be* / *to have* and the *present* / *past* participle.
2 We put the subject of the passive verb *before* / *after* the verb.

Important dates in the history of communication technology

10,000 YEARS AGO	2,000 YEARS AGO	0–100	1400s	1830s	1876
1 _smoke_	2 _bird_	Mail service	Mail service in Europe grows	The first efficient telegraph lines	3 _telephone_

12 Compare these two sentences and answer the questions.

a *Alexander Graham Bell made the first phone call in 1876.*
b *The first phone call was made in 1876.*

~~a~~ ~~b~~

1 Which sentence is active? Which is passive?
2 Which sentence focuses on the person who did the action? (a)
3 What is the focus of the other sentence? *the first phone call*
4 What happens to the object of the active sentence? *become the subject in the passive*

Check your answers on page 146. Do Exercises 1–4.

13 Match the two parts of the passive sentences.

1 The most popular smartphones and tablets
2 A smartphone is basically a mobile phone that
3 These phones are small, hand-held devices that
4 The idea of combining telephones and computers
5 But the first telephone + computer machines
6 In the 1990s these basic phones
7 By the early 2000s simple smartphones
8 Then in 2007 the first smartphone with a large screen

4 **a** was first thought of as early as 1909.
8 **b** was produced and mobile phones changed forever!
1 **c** are used all over the world today.
6 **d** were developed to send and receive emails and faxes.
3 **e** are used in a similar way to a computer.
7 **f** were sold and used in many countries.
2 **g** is connected to the internet.
5 **h** were invented in the USA in 1971.

14 Complete the article with the passive voice of the verbs. Use the present simple or past simple.

Messages from space?
The RATAN-600 radio telescope in Russia
(1) _was turned on_ (turn on) in 1974. It
(2) _was built_ (build) to receive radio signals
from space. Most of the signals are just 'space noise',
but sometimes, scientists hear radio signals with
certain patterns that they think may be messages.

In August of 2016, a signal (3) _was received_ (receive)
that was very different from the usual noise. When the
signal (4) _was shared_ (share) with experts around
the world, they agreed that it was very interesting. Was it
a message that (5) _was sent_ (send) from another
planet – a smoke signal saying *We are here*? No one knows
for sure. Every possible message (6) _is studied_ (study)
carefully, and the work continues.

15 PRONUNCIATION Stress in passive verbs

a Listen to the sentences. Underline the passive verb phrases. Which part of the verb phrase is stressed: *be*, the past participle or both? 🎧 **62**

1 An earlier message was received in the US in 1974.
2 The signal wasn't produced on Earth – it came from space.
3 Messages are sent from Earth into space every day.
4 Every time a mobile phone call is made, or a TV or radio show is broadcast, a signal is sent into space.
5 Maybe this information is studied on another planet.

b Complete the rule.

In affirmative passive verbs we usually stress
the past participle, but in negatives we stress
equally .

c Practise saying the sentences with a partner.

16 Look at these examples of technology. Write a paragraph about one of them and the ways that it is used. Use the passive.

| a computer | a pen | a smartphone |

A smartphone is used in many different ways.
First, …

17 Work in small groups. Read your paragraph to the group. Think of other ways to use the technologies your group wrote about.

A pen can be used to …

Text messages can be sent with …

Art can be created with …

The Pony Express mail service in the United States linked the East and West Coasts of the country.

1962	1973	1992	2007	The future
First email	4 _cell phone_	5 _text msg_	6 _smartphone_	7 _next big thing_

10B Can tech teach us?

VOCABULARY BUILDING Word families

> Many words have a basic form which we can use to make verbs, nouns and other parts of speech.

1 Complete the table with the other forms of the words. Use a dictionary if necessary.

Verb	Noun (thing)	Noun (person)
develop	(1)	developer
improve	(2)	–
achieve	achievement	(3)
(4)	equipment	–
disappoint	(5)	–
entertain	entertainment	(6)

2 Complete the article with words from Exercise 1.

A short history of artificial intelligence

Computer experts and software (1) _____ first began trying to create artificial intelligence (AI) in the 1950s. Their earliest (2) _____ included teaching computers to play games and do maths. They thought they could create a thinking computer within twenty years but that turned out to be a (3) _____ – the job was harder than expected. In the 1970s, work on AI slowed down, though computer games based on early research became a popular type of (4) _____ . But in the 1980s, as computer technology (5) _____ , AI research started up again. Now, companies are beginning to (6) _____ everyday technology like cars and smartphones with simple AI that can answer questions and follow spoken instructions. This means that many of us now have AI in our pocket. What will happen next?

READING

3 Read about 'chunking'. Separate the text below into chunks with slash marks (/).

> Meaning usually comes from the interaction of groups of words (chunks), not single words.
>
> When Fan Hui lost a game of Go / in October 2015, / history was made.
> about a time   who   what   when   what happened

The game of Go was invented in China more than 2,500 years ago and is one of the world's oldest – and most complicated – board games. It is played with black and white pieces called *stones* on a board with a pattern of lines.

4 Read the first paragraph of the article. Separate the chunks.

5 Read the article. Underline phrases or sentences in the article that support these ideas. Compare your answers with a partner.

1 The game between Fan Hui and AlphaGo was important.
2 Fan Hui respected AlphaGo as a player.
3 AlphaGo wasn't programmed like other computers.
4 AlphaGo learned to play Go in a way that is similar to the way a person learns.
5 AlphaGo taught Fan and Lee some new things about Go.

6 Read the article again. Choose the best option to complete each sentence.

1 AlphaGo won because it
   a copied moves made by humans.
   b made a surprising move.
   c didn't follow the rules.

2 AlphaGo
   a was programmed to win.
   b can make about three million different moves.
   c learned to play by practising.

3 Fan and Lee
   a learned from AlphaGo and became better players.
   b were very angry that AlphaGo won.
   c regret playing against AlphaGo.

CRITICAL THINKING Counterarguments

> Sometimes, when people give arguments for an idea, they don't consider arguments against the idea. Thinking about possible arguments against an idea can help us to understand it better.

7 Read the Critical thinking box. Can you think of arguments against the ideas below?

1 AIs are beautiful because they can learn, 'think' and 'feel'.
2 If AIs get smarter than humans, we can learn from them.
3 Developments in technology are a form of progress and always improve human life.

8 MY PERSPECTIVE

Think of something that you have to do that an AI could also do. How might the AI do it differently? Could you learn from this?

9 Work in pairs. Think of a problem in the world today and imagine three ways that an AI could help solve it. Make a poster explaining the technology that you imagine.

Lee Sedol (right) makes a move against AlphaGo.

ALPHAGO 01:59:50   LEE SEDOL 01:59:44

Playing against computers
THAT LEARN

🎧 63 When Fan Hui lost a game of Go in October 2015, history was made: it was the first time a human Go champion was beaten by an artificial intelligence (AI) – a computer programme that can think. And in March 2016, history was repeated when Lee Sedol – one of the world's top players – was defeated. As Fan watched AlphaGo make an important move against Lee, he thought: 'That wasn't a human move.' Then he said, 'So beautiful, so beautiful.'

Usually, game-playing electronic devices are programmed to predict the possible results of a move, but they don't learn new moves or improve. AlphaGo is different. When it was built, the AI was given three million human Go moves to analyze. Then it began playing. Through the process of sometimes losing and sometimes winning, the AI developed its own style of play, and learned to 'think' – some people even say 'feel' – like a real Go player.

Are Fan and Lee disappointed about AlphaGo's achievements? Is our technology becoming too smart? Perhaps surprisingly, the two Go champions see it as progress. After he was beaten by AlphaGo, Fan began to play the game in a different way and he improved. He won more games against other humans. Lee, whose experience was similar, said 'I have improved already. It has given me new ideas.' In this case, human and machine are working together for the development and improvement of both.

10C Using tech to take control

GRAMMAR The passive with *by* + agent

1 Read the data and the text. Then answer the questions.

> **Kenya data**
> Portion of the population who have
> • a bank account: 40%
> • access to clean drinking water: 63%
> • a mobile phone (adults): 82%

Mobile money: better than a bank

M-Pesa was started in 2007 in Kenya by Vodafone. The technology allows users to keep electronic money in their mobile phones. This money can be used to pay bills and buy things or to get cash – all without having a bank account. And now the system is used by adults who don't have a bank account in Tanzania, Afghanistan, South Africa, India, Romania and Albania.

1 Which is used by more people in Kenya: a bank account or a mobile phone?
2 How is M-Pesa used by people without a bank account?
3 Where is the system used now?
4 Who uses the system?

Passives with *by* + agent

M-Pesa was started in 2007 in Kenya **by Vodafone**.

The system is used **by adults** *who don't have a bank account …*

2 Look at the sentences in the Grammar box. Answer the questions.

1 Which form are the verbs in?
2 Who or what does the action (the agent) in the sentences?
3 How do we introduce the agent of a passive verb?
4 When do we include the agent in a passive sentence?

Check your answers on page 146. Do Exercises 5–7.

3 Work in pairs. Read the sentences. Is the agent important in each sentence or not? Cross out the agent when it isn't necessary.

1 The museum is cleaned every night by cleaners.
2 Homework is handed in each Friday by the students.
3 I was helped a lot by my friend Elliot.
4 The book was published by a publisher last year.
5 He was taught how to dive by his uncle.
6 His car was stolen by someone.

The M-Pesa programme is so successful that there are now local versions in other countries.

4 Rewrite the news headlines as full sentences in the passive.

1 Emergency services rescue British climbers in Italian Alps

British climbers in the Italian Alps were rescued by emergency services.

2 'Robot suit' helps disabled people to walk
3 Doctor uses iPad to save man's life
4 Laptop connects village in Andes Mountains to outside to world
5 Farmers use iPods to scare birds

5 Match each headline in Exercise 4 with an article (a–e).

a A Japanese company has invented a 'robot suit'. <u>Disabled people wear the device to help them to walk</u>. Strong pieces of plastic support the wearer's legs, and small motors make them move. *2*

b Two men were caught by bad weather high in the Alps near the French border with Italy. One of the men hurt his shoulder, so they had to stop climbing. They sent a text message to a friend to ask for emergency help. <u>Their friend then contacted the Italian emergency services</u>. *1*

c A US man with heart problems became ill while cycling. He asked a passing man for help, not knowing the man was a doctor. The doctor used his iPad to get information about the man's medical history and this <u>quick action, saved the man's life</u>. *3*

d In Kenya, farmers' plants are often eaten by wild animals. To frighten the animals, <u>some farmers in the Kasigau region recorded scary sounds on an iPod</u>. Electronic equipment senses when an animal is near and the iPod plays the sound, which makes the animals run away. *5*

e Children in the Andean village of Arahuay, Peru, were given laptops by the government. <u>The kids use the computers for their studies and to communicate with the outside world</u>. The government hopes the free laptops will help to educate the children. *4*

6 Look at the underlined sentences in Exercise 5. Rewrite the sentences using the passive voice. How does the passive change the focus of the sentence?

a The device …
b The emergency services …
c … the man's life …
d … scary sounds …
e The computers …

7 These sentences are all active. Would you change them into the passive? If so, rewrite the sentence and include the agent if necessary.

1 Technology is important in many schools today: children use laptops in a lot of lessons.
2 My parents don't believe that all new technology is good.
3 Someone called the emergency services and they rescued the woman from the river.
4 This mobile phone is very simple. For that reason, a lot of older people buy it.
5 Some writers, especially new ones, publish their books themselves on e-readers.

8 CHOOSE

1 Write five sentences about your favourite piece of technology. Use the passive (with *by*, where possible).

2 Work in pairs. Take turns thinking of a specific electronic device or other technology, tool or piece of equipment – something you use. Use the passive (with *by*, where possible) to describe it while your partner guesses.

3 In a small group, brainstorm an idea for a new invention. Say what it will do, who will use it and what benefits it will have. Use the passive with *by* where possible.

Young children in the village of Arahuay, Peru, use laptops at school to keep in touch with the outside world.

How to control someone else's arm with your brain

" You know, when you lose your free will, and someone else becomes your agent, it does feel a bit strange. "

GREG GAGE

Read about Greg Gage and get ready to watch his TED Talk. ▶ 10.0

AUTHENTIC LISTENING SKILLS

Reduced forms

When some words combine with *to*, some sounds are lost in speech:

going to ⟶ gonna
want to ⟶ wanna
have to ⟶ hafta

1 Listen to parts of the TED Talk where Greg Gage talks fast. You will hear each section twice. Work in pairs. Try to write down what you hear. Check your answers below. 🎧 64

1 I want to do some demonstrations. You guys want to see some?

2 So now I'm going to move away and we're going to plug it in to our human-to-human interface over here.

3 So now I'm going to hook you up over here so that you get the … It's going to feel a little bit weird at first.

2 Read the extract. Underline the expressions with *to* that you think will be reduced. Listen and check your answers. 🎧 65

So I just need to hook you up. So I'm going to find your ulnar nerve, which is probably right around here. You don't know what you're signing up for when you come up. So now I'm going to move away, and we're going to plug it in to our human-to-human interface over here.

3 Work in pairs. What do you think it would feel like to be controlled by a machine?

WATCH

4 Watch Part 1 of the talk. Choose the correct words to complete the sentences. ▶ 10.1

1 Neuroscience *is / isn't* usually taught in schools.

2 *Twenty / Fifty* percent of people have a neurological disorder at some time in their life.

3 You have 80 billion *neurons / electrical messages* in your brain.

4 When the woman squeezes her hand, we hear the sound of her *arm / brain*.

5 The green lines on the iPad show *the woman's thoughts / her brain's electrical activity*.

5 Watch Part 2 of the talk. Are the sentences true (T) or false (F)? ▶ 10.2

1 The computer will control the man's movements.

2 The signal from the woman's brain travels through the electrodes to the man's brain.

3 When the woman moves her arm the first time, the man feels nothing.

4 When the woman moves her arm again, the man's arm doesn't move.

5 When the woman's arm is moved by Greg, the man's arm moves.

6 **VOCABULARY IN CONTEXT**

a Watch the clips from the talk. Choose the correct meaning of the words and phrases. ▶ 10.3

b Look at the quote. What do the words *free will* and *agent* mean?

c Complete the sentences with your own words. Then discuss with a partner.

1 A while ago I decided to *try out* …
2 My teacher sometimes asks for a *volunteer* to …
3 Something very *weird* happened to me recently. It was …
4 A subject I find really *complex* is …

CRITICAL THINKING Analyze how a message is delivered

7 Greg thinks everyone should be able to use neuroscience technology. How does he deliver this message? Choose from a–c.

> Speakers can deliver a message in many ways. These include: providing background information or facts, demonstrating an idea or technology and comparing an idea or technology to another one. When watching a TED Talk, pay attention to how the message is being delivered. Think about why the speaker chose a certain method.

a He explains that a lot of schools have bought his equipment and that students enjoy using it.
b He gives detailed facts about how an iPad is able to show information about the brain.
c He says that his equipment is inexpensive and demonstrates that it's easy to use.
d He shows the audience that the man and woman aren't afraid of technology.
e He compares his equipment to more expensive technology and says his is better.

8 MY PERSPECTIVE

Read the questions. Take down notes.

- How could this technology be used for good? Think of three ways.
- Could it also be used for reasons that aren't good?
- If you could use the same equipment, what experiment would you like to try? What do you think the results would be?
- Is it important for new developments in communication technology to be available to everybody? Why?

9 Work in pairs. Discuss your ideas from Exercise 8. Try to think about how your partner delivers his or her message.

CHALLENGE

Greg's talk shows one of the possibilities of neuroscience, which is science about the brain and nerves. Can you think of other types of science you would like to learn more about in school? Is there technology you would like to have access to – for example, sound or video recording technology? Weather-science technology? Computer technology? Something else? How could the technology be used in class? Make notes about your idea.

In groups of four, discuss your ideas. Choose one type of technology you would like to have for your school. Then present your idea to the class. Give reasons why this technology would be helpful to learn about.

10E Who's in control?

SPEAKING

1 Companies are making cars that can drive themselves. Would you want to ride in one of these cars? Why?

2 Listen to the conversation. What pros and cons of self-driving cars are mentioned? 🎧 66

3 What other pros and cons of self-driving cars can you think of?

4 Listen again and tick (√) the expressions in the Useful language box that you hear. Then, in small groups, take turns to talk about the pros and cons of the things below. 🎧 66

- text messaging
- social media
- controlling someone else's arm with your brain
- artificial intelligence
- smartphones

5 Work in pairs. Discuss the questions.

- Does communication technology improve communication or make people communicate less?
- Does self-driving car technology make the world safer or more dangerous?
- Is technology good or bad for the environment?

Useful language

Looking at two sides of an argument

On the one hand … , (but) on the other hand …

Talking about pros

One good thing about (self-driving cars) is that …

(Self-driving cars) are good because …

Talking about cons

One bad thing about (self-driving cars) is that …

(Self-driving cars) can be a problem if / because …

Car makers say self-driving cars are safer than traditional cars.

Google

WRITING A formal letter of suggestion

6 Read the letter to the director of a leisure centre on page 153. Answer the questions.

    1 What rule is the writer of the letter unhappy about?
    2 In what ways does the writer agree with the rule?
    3 In what ways does the writer disagree with the rule?
    4 What does the writer think should happen?

7 Read the rules. What are the pros and cons of each rule?

    1 Students must not bring electronic devices to school. (Rule made by School Principal Sonja Sanchez)
    2 No music is allowed on the beach or in the park. (Rule made by Mayor Rudy Patak)
    3 Headphones cannot be worn in the leisure centre. (Rule made by Director Julia Smith)

8 **WRITING SKILL** Writing politely

    a Look at the letter on page 153 and underline the following.
        1 a polite introduction / reason for writing
        2 two ways of disagreeing politely
        3 a polite suggestion
        4 a polite ending

    b Tick (√) the expressions in the Useful language box that are also in the letter.

    c Work in pairs. Think of two possible suggestions for changing each of the rules in Exercise 7. Write the suggestions, using the expressions in the Useful language box, and write a polite introduction for a letter about each rule.

    It might be possible to allow the devices at school, but we have to switch them off during lessons.

9 Choose one of the rules in Exercise 7 and write a formal letter with at least one suggestion. Use your introductions and suggestions from Exercise 8, and the language from the Useful language box. Follow the structure of the model on page 153. Make sure you do the following.

    • say why you're writing.
    • explain the difference of opinion.
    • make a suggestion.
    • support your argument.

10 Exchange letters with a partner. Check each other's work. Does it use the language and follow the model correctly? Is it polite enough?

Useful language

Explaining differences in opinion
*While I understand that … ,
  I think / don't think …
I can see that … , but …*

Making a suggestion
*Can I suggest that …
It might be possible to …*

Supporting your argument
*(These rules) would stop … , but
  would allow …*

PRESENT SIMPLE AND PRESENT CONTINUOUS

Present simple

We use the present simple to talk about permanent states and regular habits in the present, and things that are always true.

*I'm 13 years old. I **live** in Istanbul. I **have** two sisters.*
*My school day **starts** at 8:00. I **play** football every Saturday.*
*Water **boils** at 100°C. There **are** 24 hours in a day.*

Affirmative	Negative
*I / You / We / They **drink** milk.*	*I / You / We / They **don't drink** milk.*
*He / She / It **drinks** milk.*	*He / She / It **doesn't drink** milk.*

Question	Short answer
*Do you / we / they **drink** milk?*	*Yes, I / we / they **do**.*
	*No, I / we / they **don't**.*
*Does he / she / it / **drink** milk?*	*Yes, he / she / it **does**.*
	*No, he / she / it **doesn't**.*

We form the third person singular by adding *-s* to the verb.
*He **lives** in Rome.*

When verbs end in *-o, -s, -sh, -ch, -x,* and *-z,* add *-es.*
*She **watches** football every Saturday.*

When verbs end in a consonant + *-y,* replace the *-y* with *-i* and add *-es.*
*He **studies** English.*

We form negatives and questions with *do / don't / does / doesn't* and the main verb.

Present continuous

We form the present continuous with *am / is / are + -ing* form of the main verb.

We use it to talk about things that are happening at the moment of speaking.
*I'm not **playing** football today because it**'s raining**.*

We also use the present continuous to talk about things that are happening around the time of speaking.
*I'm **reading** a good book right now.*

When a verb has one syllable and ends in a consonant, add *-ing*: *work* ⟶ *working*.

When a verb has one syllable and ends in one vowel and one consonant (but not *w, x* or *y*) we usually double the final letter: *stop* ⟶ *stopping, sit* ⟶ *sitting, plan* ⟶ *planning*

When a verb ends in *-e,* it is usually deleted when *-ing* is added.
make ⟶ *making*

Affirmative	Negative
I'm studying.	*I'm not studying.*
*You / We / They **are** studying.*	*You / We / They **aren't** studying.*
*He / She **is** studying.*	*He / She **isn't** studying.*
*It **is** raining.*	*It **isn't** raining.*

Question	Short answer
*Am I **playing**?*	*Yes, I **am**.*
	*No, I'm **not**.*
*Are you / we / they **playing**?*	*Yes, you / we / they **are**.*
	*No, you / we / they **aren't**.*
*Is he / she / it **playing**?*	*Yes, he / she / it **is**.*
	*No, he / she / it **isn't**.*

▶ Exercises 1–4

VERB PATTERNS: VERB + *-ING* OR INFINITIVE WITH *TO*

Verb + infinitive	*agree, decide, expect, hope, learn, manage, need, offer, plan, promise, seem, want, would like*
Verb + *-ing*	*avoid, can't help, consider, enjoy, finish, not mind, suggest*
Verb + *-ing* OR + infinitive	*begin, continue, hate, like, love, prefer, start*

Verb + infinitive

After some verbs, we use the infinitive form of another verb.
*I **want to be** more active.*

Verb + *-ing*

After some verbs, we use the *-ing* form of another verb.
*I **enjoy being** sociable.*

Verb + *-ing* OR + infinitive

After some verbs, we can use either form with no change in meaning. *They **like sharing** / **like to share** information.*

Questions

Form questions like this: *Does she **need to talk** to someone? What do you **want to do**? What does he **enjoy doing**?*

▶ Exercises 5–7

1 Complete the short conversations. Use the notes to write present simple questions and answers.

1 A: you / live in Argentina? *Do you live in Argentina?*
B: yes *Yes, I do.*
2 A: he / play football?
B: no
3 A: they / know Beatriz?
B: yes
4 A: we ready?
B: yes
5 A: I / late?
B: no
6 A: you / like school?
B: yes
7 A: she / study languages?
B: yes
8 A: you two / want some help?
B: no

2 Complete the sentences using the present continuous form of the verbs.

expect	get	have	stay	study	take	talk
try						

1 I _____ for my final exams.
2 My brother _____ to find a part-time job.
3 They _____ in a hotel.
4 We _____ a lot of fun!
5 You _____ a German class, right?
6 She _____ an email from her teacher.
7 I think he _____ to the new student. He's very outgoing.
8 It's pretty loud in here. I _____ a headache.

3 Choose the correct option to complete each sentence.

1 Please be quiet. We *watch / are watching* a film.
2 Phillip *plays / is playing* football every week for the school team.
3 I can't come out this evening. I *study / am studying* for the geography test.
4 What *do you do / are you doing* in the kitchen? You *make / are making* a real mess!
5 They *enjoy / are enjoying* pop music but they *don't listen / aren't listening* to it all the time.
6 It *takes / is taking* twenty minutes to get to the town centre from the school.
7 *Do you buy / Are you buying* the same fashion magazine every week?
8 We *just sit / are just sitting* at home right now because *it rains / is raining* really heavily.

4 Are the underlined verbs used correctly? If not, rewrite the sentences using the present simple or present continuous.

1 I'm knowing his first name but not his last name.
2 Do you own a bicycle?
3 We stay with friends this week.
4 They're preferring football to basketball.
5 You're learning the guitar very quickly.
6 Is she learning Spanish?
7 She's thinking about the test.
8 I finish my homework right now.

5 Choose the two options that can complete each sentence.

1 She _____ to tell me a secret.
a didn't mind   b started
c promised
2 They _____ talking to each other.
a enjoy   b like   c want
3 I _____ to learn to talk about my feelings.
a can't help   b want   c need
4 We _____ asking our mother for advice.
a prefer   b suggest   c agree
5 Can you _____ to write about your experience?
a consider   b begin   c manage
6 He _____ to believe his brother is telling the truth.
a seems   b enjoys   c wants

6 Put the words in the correct order to make sentences.

1 sister / I / my / to / hope / talk / to
2 wants / to / my / explain / feelings / me / She
3 We / emotions / mind / don't / about / talking
4 hate / You / your / sharing / feelings
5 know / would / He / to / it / like / about / more
6 My / get / lazy / she / seems / to / good / is / friend / marks / but

7 Complete the sentences with the verb in brackets. Use one -*ing* form and one infinitive form.

1 I really enjoy _____ . I want _____ a new book every week. (read)
2 I suggest _____ some new people. You can expect _____ new people by joining a club. (meet)
3 They seem _____ painting. Even when they're in a bad mood, they can't help _____ it. (enjoy)
4 He agreed _____ to the cinema with us. He didn't consider _____ out for dinner afterwards, though. (go)
5 Do you mind _____ for Ella? We need _____ about ten minutes. (wait)

PAST SIMPLE

We use the past simple:

- for completed actions and events in the past.
  We **built** the house last year.

- for actions and events in a story or series of events in the past.
  We **bought** the container on eBay and the company **delivered** it to us. We **worked** on it for six months.

- for repeated past actions and past situations.
  I **went** to the office every day.

- for past actions or events over a long period of time.
  I **grew up** in Tu Son, near Hanoi.

There are some spelling rules for regular verbs.

- for most verbs, add -ed: walk ⟶ walked
- for verbs ending in -e, add -d: like ⟶ liked
- for verbs ending in -y, change -y to -i and add -ed: try ⟶ tried; do not change the -y to -i if the verb ends in vowel + -y: play ⟶ played
- for most verbs ending in one vowel + consonant, double the final consonant and add -ed: stop ⟶ stopped; do not double the consonant if it is a w, x or y: fix ⟶ fixed

Some verbs are irregular in the affirmative form:

build ⟶ built, come ⟶ came, find ⟶ found, go ⟶ went, have ⟶ had, take ⟶ took, think ⟶ thought

The past simple of be is I/he/she/it <u>was</u> and we/you/they <u>were</u>.
It **was** a beautiful traditional house.
We **were** very happy there.

We often use time expressions with the past simple: this (morning / afternoon / evening), yesterday, last (Friday), last (week / month / year), in (2000), (two) weeks ago, when I was (a child)

Negative and questions

We form negatives in the past with *didn't* and the infinitive.
They **didn't pay** for the shipping container.

We form questions in the past with *did* and the infinitive.
Did they **move** to the city? Yes, they did.
Didn't she **buy** an old house? No, she didn't.
Where did you **live**?

We form the negative of be by adding not (n't) to the past affirmative.
It **wasn't** his house; it was hers.
They **weren't** chairs; they were old boxes.

We form questions with be by putting was / were in front of the subject.
Were they ready to leave?

Used to

We use *used to* + infinitive to talk about situations, habits and routines in the past.
They **used to live** in Mexico.

We form the negative using *didn't use to* + infinitive.
I **didn't use to go** to work every day.

We form questions with *did / didn't use to* + infinitive.
Did you **use to live** in an apartment?

▶ Exercises 1–5

PAST CONTINUOUS

We use the past continuous:

- for ongoing actions and ongoing events in the past.
  We **were walking** to school.

- for continuing situations, actions and activities in the past, especially when a single action or event happens during them.
  They **were looking** for an apartment when they discovered a houseboat.

- for past situations that continued for a long period of time.
  In 2014, he **was living** in Abu Dhabi.

We form the past continuous with the past tense of be and the present participle.

search ⟶ was/were searching, live ⟶ was / were living, work ⟶ was/were working
They **were searching** for a place to live.
We **were living** in a new house.
He **was working** in the city centre.

There are some spelling rules for forming the present participle.

- for verbs ending in a consonant, add -ing: think ⟶ thinking
- for verbs ending in -e, change -e to -ing: take ⟶ taking
- for most verbs ending in one vowel + consonant, double the final consonant and add -ing: hit ⟶ hitting

We form negative sentences with *wasn't / weren't* and the present participle.
They **weren't looking** for a house.
I **wasn't living** in Singapore.

We form questions with *was / were* and the present participle.
Were your parents **working** in Jakarta?
Wasn't she **trying** to find a new apartment?

▶ Exercises 6–8

1 Choose the correct option to complete each sentence.

1 Did you *see / saw* Beata's new house?
2 We *weren't / didn't* live in an apartment.
3 The company *was recycled / recycled* old shipping containers.
4 Where did you live when you *were / was* a child?
5 Why did your family *move / moved* to Prague?
6 Last year my brother *find / found* a really good apartment.

2 Complete the conversation with the past simple of the verbs in brackets.

A: (1) _____ (you see) the documentary on TV last night about small houses?
B: No, (2) I _____ (not). (3) _____ (be) it good?
A: Yes, it (4) _____ (be). It (5) _____ (show) people around the world living in tiny spaces – houseboats, tiny apartments. They (6) _____ (interview) a guy who (7) _____ (live) in his van at the beach.
B: Why? (8) _____ (he not have) a job?
A: Yes, he (9) _____ (do). But he (10) _____ (want) to save money. And he (11) _____ (go) surfing every day, before or after work!

3 Put the words in the correct order to make questions.

1 you / Did / the house / by yourself / build / ?
2 free / Was / container / the shipping / ?
3 a shipping container / easy / Was it / to find / ?
4 easy / to move / the container / Was it / ?
5 electricity supply / to the / you connect / Did / the house / ?

4 Complete the conversations with *used* or *use*.

A: Didn't you (1) _____ to live in Argentina?
B: No, I didn't, but my grandparents (2) _____ to live there. They lived in an apartment in Buenos Aires, and I (3) _____ to visit every summer for a few weeks.

A: We live just outside the town. We didn't (4) _____ to live in the suburbs, but now we do.
B: Where did you (5) _____ to live?
A: We (6) _____ to live in the country. It was wonderful. We (7) _____ to have a farm and horses. I didn't (8) _____ to ride them though.

5 Look at the photos above. Answer the questions.

1 What are these home furnishings now?
2 What did they use to be?

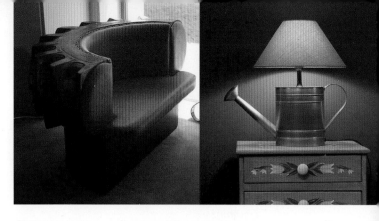

6 Write sentences in the past continuous.

1 My parents / live in Jakarta
2 We / stay in a hotel and look for a house
3 I / walk to school and think about my homework
4 They / not look for a new house
5 You / not try to sell your houseboat

7 Choose the correct option to complete each sentence.

1 My dad was working in Dubai when he *met / was meeting* my mother.
2 I *prepared / was preparing* to move away for college when I changed my plans.
3 When I was looking through some old photos, I *found / was finding* a photo of our old house.
4 While we *stayed / were staying* at my grandmother's house, my uncle visited every afternoon.

8 Complete the conversation with the past simple or past continuous of the verbs in brackets.

A: How (1) _____ (your parents find) your new apartment?
B: My dad (2) _____ (drive) to work when he (3) _____ (see) a man putting up a 'to let' sign. He (4) _____ (stop) the car right away. The man (5) _____ (drive) away, but my dad (6) _____ (shout), 'Hey, wait!', and the man (7) _____ (stop).
A: Was the man surprised?
B: Yes, but then my dad (8) _____ (ask) to see the apartment. While he (9) _____ (look) around, he (10) _____ (call) my mum and (11) _____ (tell) her to come and see it. She (12) _____ (love) it, too. So they (13) _____ (rent) it!

QUANTIFIERS

some and any

We use *some* and *any* with plural countable and uncountable nouns.

	Countable nouns	Uncountable nouns
Affirmative	He took **some** vitamins.	They drank **some** tea.
Negative	She didn't have **any** vitamins.	We didn't take **any** fish oil.
Question	Do you have **any** ideas?	Did you take **any** medicine?

We can use *some* in questions, especially when we expect the answer *yes*.

*Did they give you **some** advice?*

much, many, a lot of, a little, a few

Countable nouns
We use *a lot of* and *a few* in affirmative sentences with plural countable nouns.

***A lot of** doctors treat the whole person.*

*There are **a few** types of tea that are like medicine.*

We use *many* and *a lot of* in negative sentences and questions.

*I don't know **many** / **a lot of** natural medicines.*

*Did your doctor give you **many** / **a lot of** pills?*

Uncountable nouns
We use *a lot of* and *a little* in affirmative sentences.

*I have **a lot of** information about natural medicine.*

*There's **a little** tea in the pot.*

We use *much* and *a lot of* in negative sentences and questions.

*There isn't **much** / **a lot of** time.*

*Do you have **much** / **a lot of** work to do?*

How much? How many?

We use *How much* with uncountable nouns to ask about an amount.

***How much** information do you want?*

We use *How many* with countable nouns to ask about a number.

***How many** doctors work here?*

▶ Exercises 1–5

PHRASAL VERBS

Phrasal verbs are made up of a verb and a particle (a preposition or an adverb).

We can separate some phrasal verbs, i.e. a noun or pronoun can come between the verb and the particle. A noun can come before or after the particle, but a pronoun must come between the verb and the particle.

*Did you **write down** the information?*
*Did you **write** the information **down**?*

*His friend **picked** him **up** at six o'clock.*
~~His friend **picked up** him at six o'clock.~~

Many phrasal verbs can't be separated.

*Can you **wait for** me?*
~~Can you **wait** me **for**?~~

*Will you **look after** my bag?*
~~Will you **look** my bag **after**?~~

*His car **broke down** on the way to work.*
***Did** her car **break down** yesterday?*
*Their car **didn't break down**.*

Notice that *down* in the sentences above doesn't refer to the direction. Often, the particle doesn't have its usual meaning.

Common phrasal verbs

Inseparable
belong to, come in, complain of, deal with, eat out, get on (with someone), go in, grow up, hang out, lie down, look after, look around, look into, sit down, speak about, take off (fly), wake up, work out (at a gym)

Separable
bring back, call back, carry out (do), fill in, find out, give up, hand in, keep up, pass on, pick up, put on (clothes, music, a film), put off, take off (clothing), take up, take out, turn down, turn on, write down

▶ Exercises 6–10

1 Write the number for each noun on the correct line.

a singular countable nouns: *5,*
b plural countable nouns:
c uncountable nouns:

Before there were ¹doctors

Before modern **²science**, people used natural materials like **³plants** to cure **⁴sickness**. Older generations passed down information about the best **⁵method** for treating each **⁶illness**.

2 Choose the correct option to complete each sentence.

1 A: Do you have *any* / *many* information about going to the doctor for our school check-up?
B: No, I don't. I'm expecting to get a letter with *much* / *some* instructions.
2 A: Did the doctor give you *some* / *many* medicine?
B: No, she didn't give me *some* / *any*.
3 A: How *much* / *many* nurses work at your school?
B: There are a *little* / *few*. Three or four, I think.

3 Complete the sentences with these words.

a little	any	many	much	isn't any	some

1 I don't have _____ aspirin.
2 Sorry, but do you have _____ time to help me?
3 There are _____ flowers growing in the garden.
4 We have some milk, but not _____ .
5 How _____ plants did she write about?
6 There _____ food in the fridge – it's empty.

4 Complete the questions with *How much* or *How many*.

1 A: _____ doctors work in this hospital?
B: About 30.
2 A: _____ days were you sick?
B: Three.
3 A: _____ schoolwork did you miss?
B: A lot! I missed two tests!
4 A: _____ money do you have?
B: Sorry, I don't have any.
5 A: _____ brothers does she have?
B: Two.

5 Correct the mistake in each sentence.

1 I'm not taking ~~some~~ medicine. *any*
2 Hurry up – we don't have many time.
3 Doctors earn much money.
4 Can you give me a few advice?
5 I need a few information.
6 How much days was your holiday?

6 Complete the text with the phrasal verbs.

eat out	lie down	pick up	put on
take off	turn down		

1 When I _____ , I try to order healthy food.
2 I need to stop at the pharmacy to _____ some medicine.
3 Are you feeling OK? Maybe you should _____ .
4 Could you _____ the music? I have a headache.
5 I'm tired, so I just want to _____ a film and relax.
6 You look hot. Would you like to _____ your coat?

7 Rewrite four sentences in Exercise 6 with the verbs separated. Two sentences have inseparable phrasal verbs.

8 Put the words in order to make sentences. For separable phrasal verbs, write two answers.

1 pain / deal / do / with / How / you / ?
2 down / name / this / of / medicine / Write / the
3 carried / Who / out / research / the / ?
4 He / headache / of / complained / a
5 nurse / you / looking / Which / is / after / ?
6 this / in / form / Please / fill

9 Choose the correct particle to complete each sentence.

1 My dad looked *around* / *after* me when I was sick.
2 Everyone wants their kids to be healthy when they grow *up* / *over*.
3 It's cold. Would you like to put a sweater *on* / *off*?
4 Who does this medicine belong *for* / *to*?
5 I don't feel well. Can I lie *down* / *off*?
6 The helicopter bringing the doctor just took *up* / *off*.

10 Complete each exchange with a verb or particle.

1 A: May I speak with to Dr Chu, please?
B: He isn't here now. I'll ask him to _____ you back.
2 A: I'm really tired every day. I don't sleep well.
B: What time do you wake _____ in the morning?
A: About 4:30.
3 A: Excuse me. May I go _____ now?
B: Yes, please do. The doctor is ready to see you.
4 A: Did you find _____ what the problem was?
B: The doctor said it was a cold.
5 A: Are you OK? You look quite ill.
B: I don't feel well. Perhaps I'll _____ down for a while.

COMPARATIVES AND SUPERLATIVES

Comparative and superlative adjectives

We use comparative adjectives followed by *than* to compare two people or things. *My grandfather is **older than** my father.*

We use superlative adjectives after *the* to compare one person or thing with two or more similar people or things. *Raul is **the oldest** of my cousins.*

We form comparatives of most short adjectives with -*er*. We form superlatives of most short adjectives with -*est*.

Adjective	Comparative	Superlative
old	older	the oldest
big	bigger	the biggest
easy	easier	the easiest

Spelling rules:

*   for regular, short adjectives, add -*er* / -*est*.
    short ⟶ *shorter* ⟶ *the shortest*
*   for short adjectives ending in -*e*, add -*r* / -*st*.
    safe ⟶ *safer* ⟶ *the safest*
*   for short adjectives ending in -*y*, change the -*y* to -*i* and add -*er* / -*est*. *noisy* ⟶ *noisier* ⟶ *the noisiest*
*   for short adjectives ending in one vowel + consonant, double the final consonant and add -*er* / -*est*.
    big ⟶ *bigger* ⟶ *the biggest*

We form comparatives of most longer adjectives with *more* in front of the adjective. We form superlatives of most longer adjectives with *the most*.

Adjective	Comparative	Superlative
difficult	more difficult	the most difficult
important	more important	the most important
interesting	more interesting	the most interesting

Some adjectives have irregular forms.

Adjective	Comparative	Superlative
good	better	the best
bad	worse	the worst

▶ Exercises 1 and 2

Comparative and superlative adverbs

Comparative adverb + verb is used to compare two actions. We form comparatives of most short adverbs with -*er*.

Adverb	Comparative	Superlative
fast	faster	the fastest
late	later	the latest
slowly	more slowly	the most slowly

Some adverbs have irregular comparative and superlative forms.

Adverb	Comparative	Superlative
well	better	the best
badly	worse	the worst

▶ Exercises 3 and 4

COMPARATIVE FORMS

(not) as … as

To say how two things are similar or equal, we use *as* + adjective + *as*.

*Maths is **as difficult as** science.*

To say how one thing has less of a quality than another, i.e. isn't similar to, we use *not as* + adjective + *as*.

*The primary school is**n't as big as** the secondary school.*

too and (not) enough

We use *too* + adjective to say that the quality described is more than we want or need.

*I didn't finish my homework. It was **too difficult**.*

To make it negative, we put *not* in front of *too*.

*I finished my homework. It was**n't too difficult**.*

We use adjective + *enough* to say that the quality described is the right amount, and adjective + *not enough* to say that it isn't the right amount..

*The teacher's instructions were **clear enough**.*
*We didn't finish the project. The class was**n't long enough**.*

Expressions with *too* and *enough* often have a clause after them that gives more information about the situation. The clause starts with *to* + infinitive.

*The weather was**n't good enough to use** the kayak.*

so and such

We use *so* before an adjective to make the adjective stronger.
*My outdoor skills class was **so exciting**.*

We use *such* before an adjective + noun to make the combination stronger.
*I had **such a good science teacher** last year.*

So and *such* can also have a clause after them which shows the result of the action in the first clause. This clause starts with *that*.

*My outdoor skills class was **so exciting that** I decided to stay for another hour.*

▶ Exercises 5–7

1 Write sentences with comparatives that give your opinion.

1 studying / watching TV (enjoyable)
I think *studying is more enjoyable than watching TV* ?

2 languages / science (important)
I think _____ .

3 reading / writing (hard)
I think _____ .

4 information on the internet / information in books (interesting)
I think _____ .

5 speaking / listening (easy)
I think _____ .

6 studying late at night / studying early in the morning (good)
I think _____ .

2 Complete the sentences with the superlative form of the adjectives in brackets.

1 _____ (hard) part of the school year is final exams.

2 For me, _____ (bad) part of PE is running.

3 _____ (important) subject in primary school these days is information technology.

4 Friday is _____ (good) day of the week.

5 English is _____ (popular) foreign language.

6 In my school, _____ (big) class has eighty students in it.

3 Put the words in the correct order to make sentences.

1 than at night / I study / in the morning / better

2 more quickly than / Davina finished / I did / the science exam

3 than the other / on the project / harder / groups / Our group worked

4 his maths test / than in / He did worse / in his science test

5 learned French / faster than / They learned German / they

6 more slowly / the teacher / I asked / to speak

4 Complete the sentences with the superlative form of the adverbs.

badly	fast	hard	late	slowly	well

1 A: I have a test tomorrow. How can I learn a list of vocabulary words *the fastest* ?
B: You should try flash cards. But you learn _____ by studying a little bit every day for several weeks.

2 A: The heavy rain caused a lot of traffic delays. Who arrived at school _____ ?
B: I did. I think my bus driver drove _____ .

3 A: I work _____ in maths, because it's the most difficult subject.
B: Me, too. I always do _____ in maths tests. I never get good marks.

5 Write sentences with (*not*) *as … as* that are true for you.

1 playing sports / watching TV (relaxing)
2 taking a test / writing an essay (stressful)
3 school lunch / lunch at home (tasty)
4 the weekend / weekdays (busy)
5 walking / taking the bus (enjoyable)
6 speaking English / reading English (easy)

6 Complete the second sentence in each pair with the words in brackets.

1 I don't have the right amount of time to do my homework. (enough)
I don't have _____ to do my homework.

2 The weather wasn't dry enough to play outside. (too wet)
The weather was _____ outside.

3 There's the right amount of space in the classroom for two more desks. (enough)
There's _____ .

4 The exam wasn't easy enough for me to complete in an hour. (too difficult)
The exam _____ .

5 Was there the right number of textbooks for the whole class? (enough)
Were there _____ ?

6 We aren't tall enough to join the basketball team. (too short)
We're _____ .

7 Complete the sentences with *so* or *such*.

1 That was _____*such*_____ an interesting lesson.
That lesson was _____ interesting.

2 The test was _____ difficult.
It was _____ a difficult test.

3 The assignment was _____ long that I couldn't finish it.
It was _____ a long assignment that I couldn't finish it.

4 It was _____ a good outdoor skills course that I wanted to do it again.
The outdoor skills course was _____ good that I wanted to do it again.

PRESENT PERFECT AND PAST SIMPLE

Present perfect

We use the present perfect to talk about experiences or things that happened in the past without saying exactly when they happened.

We use the present perfect for:

- actions in the past with a result in the present.
  I've lost my keys and can't get into my house.
- situations that started in the past and continue to now.
  We've always lived in this house.
- experiences that happened at an unspecified time.
  She's travelled to Canada several times.

We form the present perfect with *have / has* + the past participle of the main verb.

I've travelled to Asia.

We add *not* or *never* to talk about experiences that haven't happened.

I haven't travelled to South America. / I've never travelled to South America.

Affirmative	Negative
I / You / We / They **have travelled** a long way.	I / You / We / They **haven't travelled** a long way.
He / She / It **has travelled** a long way.	He / She / It **hasn't travelled** a long way.

Question	Short answer
Have I / you / we / they **travelled** a long way?	Yes, I / you / we / they **have**.
	No, I / you / we / they **haven't**.
Has he / she / it **travelled** a long way?	Yes, he / she / it **has**.
	No, he / she / it **hasn't**.

ever, never, and *always*

We add *ever* before the participle in a question to mean *in your whole life*.

*Have you **ever** tried Indonesian food?*

We use *never* in a statement to say *not in my whole life*.

*I've **never** been to Peru.*

Never is not usually used in questions.

~~Have you never been to China?~~
A: *Have you **ever** been to China?*
B: *No, I've **never** been to China.*

We use *always* to say that a situation has continued your whole life.

*We've **always** lived in this house.*

Present perfect and past simple

When we use the present perfect, exactly when the action happened is not usually given. When we want to say exactly when something happened, we use the past simple.

*You've **met** my cousin. You **met** her last year at my party.*

Notice that *been* can be the past participle of both *be* and *go*.

*I've **been** really busy this week. (= be)*
*Mum's **been** to Italy on business a few times. (= go)*

▶ Exercises 1–4

PRESENT PERFECT WITH *FOR, SINCE, ALREADY, JUST* AND *YET*

Present perfect with *for* and *since*

Use *for* to talk about how long something has gone on.

*I've **known** Layla **for** four years.*

Use *since* to talk about when something began.

*He's **lived** with his uncle **since** 2016.*

Present perfect with *just, already* and *yet*

With the present perfect, we use:

- *just* to talk about something very recent. *Just* always goes before the participle.
  *We've **just heard** a very funny joke.*
  ***Have** you **just arrived**?*
- *already* to talk about something that happened before now, without saying when. *Already* usually comes before the participle.
  *They're not here – they've **already left**.*
  ***Has** he **already gone** to bed?*

  But in US English it can come after the participle.
  ***Has** he **gone** to bed **already**?*
- *yet* to talk about something that hasn't happened but is expected to happen. *Yet* comes at the end of the clause.
  *I **haven't met** your parents **yet**.*
  ***Has** your cousin **arrived yet**?*

▶ Exercises 5–8

1 Complete the questions with the present perfect of the verbs.

go	kiss	meet
play	see	take

1 ___Have___ you ever _____ to a big wedding?
2 _____ Michaela _____ the car?
3 _____ Erika _____ your new house?
4 _____ your brother _____ football with my friend Jakob?
5 _____ your grandparents ever _____ you?
6 _____ I _____ your uncle before?

2 Complete these answers. Then match each answer with a question in Exercise 1.

a No, she _____ . Ricardo took it to go to work. *2*
b Yes, of course they _____ – every time I've visited them!
c Yes, I _____ . I have a lot of older cousins, so I've been to five or six huge ones.
d No, you _____ . That was my older brother.
e Yes, he _____ . They've played together a few times.
f No, she _____ . I haven't invited her over yet.

3 Complete the conversation with one word in each space.

A: Have you (1) _____ been abroad on holiday?
B: Yes, I (2) _____ . I (3) _____ to Turkey last year.
A: You're lucky. I've (4) _____ been out of the country.
B: (5) _____ you had holidays here, though?
A: Oh, yes. My aunt and uncle live in the mountains, and my family (6) _____ stayed with them a few times.
B: That's great. I (7) _____ been to the mountains. I've love to go.
A: Well, my uncle (8) _____ bought an apartment there. Perhaps your family could rent it.

4 Correct the mistake in each sentence.

1 ~~Have you seen~~ your cousins when you were in Dubai last week? *Did you see*
2 I didn't ever go to a wedding.
3 They never met my best friend. This will be the first time.
4 Has he enjoyed the celebration last night?
5 We've missed an exciting celebration yesterday.
6 My sister is only twelve, but she learned three foreign languages.

5 Put the words in order to make sentences.

1 gone / Sarah / just / has / out
2 primary school / known / We've / since / each other
3 I / seen / Jaime / yet / haven't
4 for / rained / hasn't / It / three weeks
5 that / already / film / seen / We've

6 Choose the correct word to complete each sentence.

1 Have you been friends *for / since* a long time?
2 They've had the same teacher *for / since* three years.
3 So you've lived in Singapore *for / since* 2010?
4 Her grandmother has called every year on her birthday *for / since* Layla was born.
5 You've been my next-door neighbour *for / since* my whole life.
6 We've made each other laugh *for / since* the first time we met.

7 Complete the sentences with the present perfect of the verbs in brackets and *for* or *since*.

1 My cousin _____ (live) in Madrid _____ fifteen years.
2 They _____ (know) Ed _____ he was a baby.
3 We _____ (be) friends _____ primary school.
4 You _____ (have) the same friends _____ ten years.
5 I _____ (not see) you _____ last summer.
6 I _____ (meet) him every Friday _____ three months.

8 Complete the conversations with the words given.

1 already / yet
A: Have you _____ met your new neighbour?
B: No, not _____ .
2 yet / just
A: I've _____ seen Rory.
B: Oh, really? I haven't seen him _____ .
3 already / just
A: I've _____ had lunch. Have you?
B: Yes, I've _____ eaten.
4 just / yet
A: I haven't celebrated my fifteenth birthday _____ . Has your brother?
B: Yes, he's _____ celebrated it. His birthday was last week.

MODAL VERBS: OBLIGATION, PROHIBITION, PERMISSION, ADVICE

must, have to

We use *must* and *have to* + the infinitive of a verb to say that something is very important or is necessary – an obligation.

We use *must* when the speaker thinks something is important.

*You **must** remember to call David.*

We often use *have to* when someone else has made a decision or rule.

*I **have to** hand in my homework by 3:00.*

We usually use *have to* to ask if something is necessary.

*Do I **have to** buy a ticket?*

Questions with *must* are grammatically correct, but can sound old-fashioned or formal.

***Must** I buy a ticket?*

mustn't and can't

We use *mustn't* + infinitive to express prohibition, i.e. to say that something is not allowed, or to say that it is very important <u>not</u> to do something.

*You **mustn't** enter this part of the building. (It isn't allowed.)*

*You **mustn't** wear shoes in the temple. (It's very important that you don't wear shoes.)*

We use *can't* + infinitive to express prohibition.

*You **can't** park here. (It isn't allowed.)*

Mustn't sounds stronger and more formal than *can't*. We can use *must not*, with both parts stressed, for stronger prohibition.

can and don't have to

We use *have to* to ask about what's necessary or allowed.

*Do I **have to** arrive at 8:00?*

We use *don't have to* + infinitive to show:

* that something isn't important or necessary.
  *You **don't have to** wear shoes here. (But it's OK if you want to wear shoes.)*
* that you can choose not to do something.
  *You **don't have to** come to the meeting – it's optional.*

We use *can* + infinitive to give permission.

*You **can** use this computer to check your email. (It's allowed.)*

We use *can* to ask for permission.

***Can** I use my phone here? (Is it allowed?)*

should and shouldn't

We use *should* and *shouldn't* + infinitive to give advice, i.e. to say that it is or isn't a good idea to do something.

*You **should** hire a private tour guide at the museum. You'll learn more that way.*

*You **shouldn't** go on a group tour – it's too noisy.*

Should is also used to ask for advice.

***Should** I take my camera?*

When *shouldn't* is used in a question, it suggests that the speaker thinks the answer is already known.

*I'm sure it's going to rain. **Shouldn't** you take an umbrella?*

▶ Exercises 1–4

ZERO CONDITIONAL

We use the zero conditional to talk about facts and things that are generally true.

*If / **When** you practise, you improve.*

*If / **When** you don't practise, you don't improve.*

We form the zero conditional with two present simple clauses. One clause uses *if* or *when*. The other expresses a result of the action in the *if / when* clause.

If / When clause	Result clause
If / When + present simple	present simple

Either clause can come first.

*You can't succeed **if / when** you don't try.*

*If / **When** you don't try, you can't succeed.*

When the *if / when* clause is at the start of the sentence, it is separated from the main clause with a comma.

We can use *if* + present simple as an imperative to give advice or instructions.

If you see a painting by Banksy, take a picture of it.

Don't forget to visit some art galleries when you go Buenos Aires.

▶ Exercises 5–8

1 Choose the best option to complete the sentences.

1 You *don't have to / can't* use your phone here. It's against the rules.
2 According to the rules, you *shouldn't / have to* say how old you are when you sign up for a social media account.
3 *Should / Can't* I wear a tie on Friday evening? Is it formal?
4 You *must / mustn't* return the library book by Friday.
5 We *mustn't / should* wear shoes here. We have to take them off.
6 *Have to / Can* I wear these boots to school?
7 You *can / shouldn't* wear that old T-shirt to school – it's too dirty.
8 We *don't have to / have to* dress up for the party – it's casual.

2 Put the words in the correct order to make sentences.

1 uniform / you / Do / wear / a / to / have / ?
2 arrive / must / We / for / on time / class / the
3 can't / You / this / computer / use
4 can't / midnight / after / They / phone / the / use
5 to / this / for / have / pay / we / Do / ?
6 we / wait / Shouldn't / Alex / for / ?

3 Look at the signs. Complete the sentences with *must*, *mustn't*, *don't have to*, *can*, *can't* and *should*.

1	2	3	4	5	6
					STOP

1 You ___can___ ride a bicycle on this road.
2 You _____ go at exactly 50 kilometres per hour, but you mustn't drive faster.
3 You _____ eat or drink here.
4 You _____ drive slowly as there are children around here.
5 You _____ use your phone here.
6 You _____ stop.

4 Correct the mistake in each sentence.

1 You ~~haven't to~~ wear a tie. *don't have to*
2 I don't must forget my jacket.
3 You not have to pay – it's free.
4 They don't have to park there. It's illegal.
5 You should to change your shirt.
6 Children don't have to use the library. It's open to everyone.

5 Match the two parts of the sentences.

1 Artists like it
2 It can hurt
3 You should ask permission
4 Artists sell their work
5 We learn a lot
6 Tourists look out for street art

a if people say they don't like one of your paintings.
b if they become well known.
c when people travel to see their work.
d when they visit big cities.
e when you want to paint in a public space.
f when we make mistakes.

6 Make zero conditional sentences using the information.

1 I have time / I paint
When _____ .
2 it can be beautiful / something is imperfect
If _____ .
3 we learn from them / we make mistakes
When _____ .
4 we practise / we develop our skills
If _____ .
5 you relax / you enjoy your work more
When _____ .

7 Use the words to write sentences with *you* + the present simple tense.

1 If / want / learn about painting / take a class.
2 Try / see some street art / when / go to Paris.
3 If / need / finish something / accept imperfection.
4 Ask for help / aren't sure what to do.
5 If / have time / visit the art galleries.

8 Complete the conversation with the verbs.

can find	get	go	google	know
try				

A: When you (1) _____ to Warsaw next month, (2) _____ to see some street art.
B: Is there a lot of street art in Warsaw?
A: If you (3) _____ where to look, you (4) _____ it.
B: So where should I look?
A: When you (5) _____ 'Warsaw street art', you (6) _____ a list of art and artists.

PREDICTIONS AND ARRANGEMENTS

Predictions with *will*

Affirmative	Negative
I / You / He / She / It / We / They **will eat**.	I / You / He / She / It / We / They **won't eat**. (won't = will not)

Question	Short answer
Will I / you / he / she / it / we / they **eat?**	**Yes**, I / you / he / she / it / we / they **will**. **No**, I / you / he / she / it / we / they **won't**.

We use *will* + infinitive for predictions that we are certain about.
It **will be** good fun!

We also use *will* + infinitive for immediate decisions.
I'll go to the shop.

We form negative sentences with *won't* (*will not*) + infinitive.
*We **won't have** a problem feeding everyone.*

We form questions with *will* + subject + infinitive.
***Will** we **grow** food underwater?*

Predictions with *might* and *may*

We use *might* or *may* + infinitive to talk about possible future events or situations. *Might / may* are less certain than *will*.
*We **might discover** new sources of food.*
*The population **may not increase** so quickly.*

Future with *going to*

We use (*be*) *going to* + infinitive to talk about plans or predictions.
*I'm **going to be** in cookery school next year. It's **going to be** a lot of work.*

going to or *will*?

Going to is usually used when there is evidence for a prediction, especially when it is expected to happen soon.
*I invited three friends for dinner, so we'**re going to need** more food!*

Will is usually used for long-term predictions or when we make a prediction from our previous experience.
*The world population **will be** about 10 billion in 2050. He'**ll be** late – he always is.*

In many cases, there is no difference between *will* and *going to* for predictions.

Present continuous for future arrangements

We can use the present continuous to talk about plans for the future.
*We'**re meeting** after school today.*

In many cases, there is no difference between using the present continuous and *going to* when talking about future plans, but we often use the present continuous when the arrangement involves other people.
*We'**re going to give** our presentation next Monday.*
*We'**re giving** our presentation next Monday.*

When talking about future plans, we usually use a future time expression with the present continuous.
*I'**m working** on my project <u>next week</u>. (= future)*
*I'**m working** on my project. (= now)*

▶ Exercises 1–6

FIRST CONDITIONAL

We use the first conditional to talk about a possible or likely future. The *if* clause explains what must happen (the condition) for the future result in the main clause.
If you go to China, you'll eat a lot of delicious food.

The *if* clause can be in two places. Notice the comma when the *if* clause comes first.
*You'll meet some farmers **if** you visit the countryside.*
***If** you visit the countryside, you'll meet some farmers.*

We form the first conditional with *if* + present simple and *will / won't* + infinitive in the result clause.
*If we **don't allow** large signs on the street, businesses owners **will be** angry.*

may, might, could

May, *might* and *could* can be used instead of *will* when possible events are less certain.
*If you travel the world, you **may** discover foods you never knew about.*
*You **might** eat fish for breakfast if you go to Japan.*
*If you travel in Brazil, it **could** be difficult to find vegetarian food.*

When

For situations in the future, *when* is used to show that a speaker is sure something is going to happen.
***When** you go to Korea, you might eat bulgogi. (You're definitely going to Korea.)*
***If** you go to Korea, you might eat bulgogi. (There's a possibility you're going to Korea, but I'm not sure you're going.)*

▶ Exercises 7–10

1 Complete the sentences with *will* or *'ll*.

1 Food _____ be more expensive.
2 We _____ eat less meat.
3 Robots _____ work on farms.
4 Some people _____ have food 'printers' in their kitchen.
5 _____ people grow more vegetables at home?

2 Put the words in the correct order to make predictions.

1 may / We / more / grow / in / food / laboratories
2 will / There / people / be / more / a lot
3 there / Will / fish / enough / be / ?
4 be / What / the / population / will / ?
5 eat / They / fast / won't / food

3 Complete the sentences with *(not) going to*.

1 Look at the clouds. it *'s going to* rain on our picnic!
2 There's too much food. We _____ finish it.
3 There are two pizzas for ten people. _____ we _____ have enough food for everyone?
4 This restaurant is very unpopular, so it _____ close.
5 The cost of raising animals is increasing. _____ meat _____ become more expensive?

4 Complete the sentences with *going to* and the verbs in brackets.

1 _____ a vegetarian diet _____ (be) more popular in the future?
2 People _____ (eat) more plants that grow in the sea.
3 The typical home _____ (have) a big vegetable garden.
4 _____ restaurants _____ (serve) more local food?
5 I _____ (not change) my way of eating.

5 Match these situations with the predictions or questions in Exercise 4.

a People are becoming more interested in growing their own food.
b When they eat out, people want to know where the food comes from.
c A lot of people avoid meat these days.
d I know what I like to eat.
e The Japanese diet includes a lot of seaweed.

6 Write sentences using *will* or *going to*.

1 In the next 50 years / people live on Mars
2 By the year 2100 / most of our food come from factories
3 People like healthy food / so fast food be less popular
4 Farming is difficult / fewer people become farmers
5 After we end the problem of hunger / the world be a better place

7 Put *will* in the correct place in each sentence.

1 If we have enough farms, we *will* be able to feed everyone.
2 You have delicious honey if you visit Kars.
3 If they leave their villages, people forget their traditions.
4 If I make a salad, you stay and have dinner with us?
5 Hannah teach us some recipes if we ask her?

8 Choose the correct option to complete each sentence.

1 If the bees don't transfer the pollen, fruit *will / won't* grow.
2 These plants don't like water, so they *might / might not* be healthy if you give it to them every day.
3 If we *don't meet / meet* any beekeepers, I'll buy some honey.
4 If we act now, we *may / may not* be able to save the bees.

9 Complete the sentences with the correct form of the words in brackets.

1 If you _____*choose*_____ (choose) the restaurant, I *'ll make* _____ (make) the reservation.
2 We _____ (see) each other tomorrow if we _____ (not meet) tonight.
3 If they _____ (leave) home at 7:00, they _____ (arrive) at the restaurant at 7:30.
4 He _____ (bring) some food with him if you _____ (ask) him to.
5 You _____ (be) hungry later on if you _____ (not take) enough food with you.
6 If you _____ (want) to do the homework together, I _____ (come) to your place after dinner.

10 Read the sentences. Write conditional sentences with the words in brackets.

1 I want to try the new vegetarian restaurant. I might have time. (will / if)

   I'll try the new vegetarian restaurant if I have time.

2 They want to buy some Turkish honey. They might find it in town. (may / if)
3 The bees might be happy. Happy bees make a lot honey. (if / might)
4 He will finish reading the book. He will know more about bees. (when / will)
5 It's possible for her to interview a beekeeper. She might find one. (might / if)

SECOND CONDITIONAL

We use the second conditional to talk about imaginary, unlikely or impossible situations. The *if* clause explains what is necessary for the result in the main clause.

*If I **had** more time for shopping, I'**d be** really happy.*
(= I don't have time for shopping.)

*If I **had** more money, I'**d buy** some new clothes.*
(= I don't have more money.)

*If I **were** taller, this shirt **would fit**.*
(= I am a certain height, and I can't change that.)

We form the second conditional with *if* + past simple and *would / wouldn't* + infinitive in the result clause.

*If I **were** you, I **would buy** the recycled cotton bag.*

Notice that the verb in the *if* clause is in the past simple even though the sentence refers to the present or the future.

The *if* clause can appear in two places. When the *if* clause begins a sentence, we separate it from the main clause with a comma.

*If you **had** a SellMyStuff account, you **could sell** some of your old things.*

*You **could sell** some of your old things if you **had** a SellMyStuff account.*

We usually use *would* in the result clause, but to emphasize that something is just a possibility, *could* or *might* can be used.

*If I **bought** this and didn't like it, I **could give** it to you.*

*If it **weren't** too small, I **might buy** it.*

Notice that when we are talking about imaginary or impossible conditions, we can use *were* after *I*, *he*, *she* and *it*.

*If he **was / were** here now, he would tell you about it.*

▶ Exercises 1–2

The second conditional is different from the first conditional. We use the first conditional to talk about a possible or likely future event. We use the second conditional to talk about an imaginary, unlikely or impossible future event.

First conditional: *If I find any old clothes, I'll put them in the recycling bin.* (= likely)

Second conditional: *If I found any old clothes, I'd put them in the recycling bin.* (= unlikely) OR *If I had any old clothes, I'd put them in the recycling bin.* (= imaginary, I don't have any old clothes.)

▶ Exercises 3–5

DEFINING RELATIVE CLAUSES

A defining relative clause gives information about the noun that comes directly before it and says exactly who or what the noun is. In defining relative clauses we use the relative pronouns *who*, *that* and *which*.

*The **shop that** sells second-hand furniture is near here.*

*The **person who** sold me this shirt also made it.*

*Advertisements **which** don't tell the truth are terrible.*

The relative clause can define either the subject of the main clause (as in the examples above) or the object of the main clause.

*I know the **person who** made this shirt.*

*I hate **advertisements that** don't tell the truth.*

In all of the above sentences, the relative pronoun has to be included because in each case it is the subject of the relative clause.

~~This is the shop sells beautiful upcycled lamps.~~

If the relative pronoun is the object of the verb in the relative clause, the relative pronoun can be left out.

*These are the new shoes **that** I told you about.*

These are the new shoes I told you about.

We use the relative pronouns in the following ways:

- *who* identifies people.
  *The **guy who** runs the restaurant grows his own vegetables.*
- *which* identifies things.
  *I couldn't find a **shop which** sold the kind of clothes I like to buy.*
- *that* identifies people and things. Using it this way is less formal than *who* or *which*.
  *The **artist that** made this lamp lives in Madrid. The **work that** he does is really interesting.*

We can also use defining relative clauses to join two sentences together.

This is a table. It used to be a traffic sign.

*This is a table **that** used to be a traffic sign.*

▶ Exercises 6–9

1 Put *would* in the correct place in each sentence.

1 You see happy workers if you visited the factory.
2 If they designed cool clothes, people buy them.
3 If I gave you this shirt, you wear it?
4 David wear his new jacket if he came to the party?

2 Put the words in the correct order to make sentences.

1 sell anything / we wouldn't / If we / advertise / didn't
2 your old clothes, / If you didn't / you could / throw away / recycle them
3 grow soy / They would / didn't grow corn / if they
4 would sell / The shop / if it were / more / bigger
5 a coat, / you could / If / make it / I designed

3 Write second conditional sentences using *if* and the words in brackets.

1 He loves designing clothes. That's why he does it. (wouldn't)

He wouldn't design clothes if he didn't love it.

2 I don't have any money. I can't buy new clothes. (had)
3 You probably have some money. If not, I could pay for these shoes. (didn't)
4 It might rain tomorrow. We might not go swimming. (wouldn't)
5 She has to work tomorrow. She won't go shopping. (didn't)

4 Choose the correct option to complete each sentence.

1 If I have time on Saturday, I *would / will* go shopping.
2 We'd buy our clothes at a recycled clothes store if our town *had / has* one.
3 Will you *waited / wait* for me outside the store if I'm a few minutes late?
4 She wouldn't buy from this company if they *don't / didn't* pay their workers well.
5 If the billboards weren't here, this street *would look / looks* much better.

5 Complete the sentences with the present simple, past simple or the *will* or *would* form of the verb.

1 If I buy the blue jacket, I ___won't buy___ (not buy) the red one.
2 Gregor will answer your questions if you _____ (have) any.
3 If you _____ (not care) about the workers, would you buy cheaper clothes?
4 How would you feel if you _____ (work) in a dangerous clothing factory?
5 What _____ (you / do) if you can't find a shirt you like?
6 I _____ (not choose) that colour if I were you.

6 Choose the correct option.

1 I want to buy a jacket *who / that* isn't too expensive.
2 Is this the shop *which / who* sells old computers?
3 They're the guys *which / who* design the skateboards.
4 The person *which / that* made this chair also designs clothes.
5 Do you know a shop *that / who* sells good used clothes?
6 My friend *which / who* runs his own shop lives in Rio.

7 Match the two parts of the sentences.

1 The shop
2 I bought this shirt in a town
3 She's the person
4 Six is the time
5 He designed the clothes
6 They're the people

a which isn't far from Paris.
b that the shops close.
c who turn old clothes into handbags.
d that I wore last week.
e which I love is over there.
f who makes upcycled furniture.

8 Look at the table. Write sentences using relative pronouns.

Person or thing	What the person or thing is	Important information
1 Mr Han	college teacher	teaches furniture design
2 Old to New	shop	sells upcycled furniture
3 Di Garcia	designer	designed my shirt
4 China Square Central	shopping centre in Singapore	has a weekend market for selling used things
5 The Sato family	our neighbours	own several clothing shops

1 Mr Han is a college teacher who teaches furniture design.

9 Combine the sentences in two ways. Use *that* or *who*.

1 I bought a jacket. It was made by hand.

The jacket I bought was made by hand.
I bought a jacket that was made by hand.

2 We saw a lamp. It used to be a coffee can.
3 We know a designer. He made my desk.
4 I bought a table. It wasn't expensive.

PAST PERFECT

We use the past perfect to talk about completed actions that happened before a certain time in the past.

worked in Spain ⟶ worked in Peru ⟶ moved to the US

He'**d worked** in Spain and Peru before he **moved** to the US.

We form the past perfect with *had* + the past participle.

She'**d lived** in Rio for ten years before she moved to Fortaleza.

Affirmative	Negative
I / You / He / She / It / We / They **had arrived** on schedule.	I / You / He / She / It / We / They **hadn't arrived** on schedule.

Yes / No questions	Short answers
Had I / you / he / she / it / we / they **arrived** on schedule?	Yes, I / you / he / she / it / we / they **had**.
	No, I / you / he / she / it / we / they **hadn't**.

These time expressions can be used with the past perfect: *already, before, by the time, just, yet*

They **had already started** class when she arrived.

He **hadn't studied** computer science **before** he went to college.

By the time she was twenty-two years old, she **had written** three books.

I'**d just moved** to Madrid when I met Marco.

When you got your job, **had** you **finished** college **yet**?

Past perfect and past simple

We often use the past perfect with the past simple to talk about actions or situations that happened before a more recent action.

I **had been** on the boat for less than two hours when we **saw** our first whale.

Notice that with the conjunction *after* we can use either the past simple or the past perfect.

I got a job immediately after I **left** college.

I got a job immediately after I **had left** college.

▶ Exercises 1–4

REPORTED SPEECH

To say what another person said, we use reported speech. In reported speech, the verb tense is usually moved backwards in time and pronouns, possessive adjectives, and adverbs of time and place are also changed.

The most common reporting verb is *said*. We can use *that* after *said*, but we often leave it out.

Tense changes in statements

Actual words		Reported speech
present simple 'You're a good writer.'	⟶	past simple *He said (that) I was a good writer.*
present continuous 'You're going to graduate.'	⟶	past continuous *They said (that) I was going to graduate.*
past simple 'Her performance showed natural ability.'	⟶	past simple / past perfect *She said (that) her performance showed / had shown natural ability.*
present perfect 'You've worked very hard.'	⟶	past perfect *He said (that) I'd worked very hard.*
will / won't 'You'll be famous one day.' 'You won't forget your friends.'	⟶	would / wouldn't *She said (that) I would be famous one day.* *She said (that) I wouldn't forget my friends.*
can / can't 'I can help you.' 'I can't do your work for you.'	⟶	could *He said (that) he could help me.* *He said (that) he couldn't do my work for me.*

said and *told*

We always use an object with *told*.

'I'm your new teacher.'	⟶	He told us / me / them / you (that) he was our new teacher. ~~He told (that) he was our new teacher.~~

We never use an object with *said*.

'I'm your new teacher.'	⟶	He said (that) he was our new teacher. ~~He said us / me / them / you (that) he was our new teacher.~~

In reported speech, the words that refer to people, times and places need to be changed.

I	⟶ *he / she / it / you*
you	⟶ *I / we*
we	⟶ *you / they*
my	⟶ *his / her / its / your*
our	⟶ *your / their*
now	⟶ *then*
today	⟶ *that day*
tomorrow	⟶ *the next day*
yesterday	⟶ *the day before / the previous day*
last / next	⟶ *the last / the next*
last night	⟶ *the night before / the previous night*
here	⟶ *there*
this room	⟶ *that room*

▶ Exercises 5–7

1 Complete the article with the past simple or past perfect of the verbs in brackets.

An early love for the ocean

Asha de Vos was born and grew up in Sri Lanka. As a baby, she loved the water and (1) _____ (learn) to swim by the time she was three. And by the age of six, she (2) _____ (decide) to become a marine biologist when she grew up.

A job on a potato farm

When she graduated from university in Scotland, Asha (3) _____ (take) a job working on a potato farm. Although she had tried during her final year of university, she (4) _____ (not be) able to find a job in marine biology, and now she (5) _____ (need) money because she (6) _____ (already decide) to travel to New Zealand to work on conservation projects – which she eventually (7) _____ (do).

Finding a career in marine biology

After she (8) _____ (work) for six months in New Zealand, she (9) _____ (get) a job on a research boat and travelled the world's oceans, looking at whales. Eventually, she (10) _____ (go) back to university and earned a PhD in marine biology. Now she's building a marine conservation research and education centre in Sri Lanka to share her love of the ocean with others.

---

2 Look at the article in Exercise 1. Write questions using the verbs in brackets. Use the past perfect or past simple.

1 When _____ (you decide) to become a marine biologist?
2 _____ (you try) to find a biology job before you finished university?
3 Why _____ (you take) a job on a potato farm?
4 How long _____ (you be) in New Zealand before you got the research job?
5 What did you do after _____ (you get) your PhD?

3 Complete the answers to the questions in Exercise 2. Use the past perfect where you can.

1 By the age of six I … *had decided to become a marine biologist.*
2 Yes, I …
3 I realized that I needed money because …
4 I got the research job when I …
5 After I …

4 Look at the underlined verbs. Do they use the past perfect correctly? Correct the ones with mistakes.

1 When he called me, I hadn't answered the phone.
2 She talked to the careers adviser and had asked for some advice.
3 They were expecting us because we had emailed and told them were coming.
4 I texted you this morning. Had you got it?
5 When I went to her office, she had gone, so we didn't talk.

5 Complete the reported speech.

1 'Your work is excellent.'
   She said that _____ excellent.
2 'I learned a lot from your presentation.'
   He told _____ a lot from my presentation.
3 'They've worked hard on their performance.'
   She said that _____ on their performance.
4 'We'll be happy to help you.'
   He told _____ to help me.
5 'I want to go to college.'
   She said that _____ to college.

6 Write the reported sentences in direct speech.

1 He said he would see me the next week.
2 She said she was interested in languages.
3 She said they'd started learning kung fu last year.
4 He said you practised every day.
5 She said she would get a job to pay for college.

7 Read the conversation. Complete the reported speech below.

Davina: I want to study art in college.
Ben: Why do you want to do that?
Davina: I really enjoyed my art class last year.
Ben: What did you like about it?
Davina: It taught me to see. I've discovered a new side of myself!
Ben: Will your parents let you study art?
Davina: I'm not sure, but it can't hurt to ask them.

Davina said (1) _____ to study art in college. She said she (2) _____ her art class (3) _____ year. She said it (4) _____ her to see. She (5) _____ a new side of herself. Ben asked if her parents would let her study art. Davina said that it (6) _____ to ask them.

THE PASSIVE

We use the passive when the person who does the action (the agent) is obvious, unimportant or unknown.

object

Active: *Scientists develop new technology every day.*

Passive: *New technology **is developed** every day.*

subject

The passive focuses attention on the object of the verb: new technology. The object of the active verb becomes the subject of the passive verb.

Present simple passive

We form the present simple passive with the present of *be* + the past participle of the main verb. We use the present simple passive for:

- facts that are generally true.
  *A lot of electronic devices **are made** in China.*

- regular actions.
  *Diving classes **are held** every Saturday.*

- steps in a process.
  *The devices **are designed** in California. After they're **built** in China, they're **shipped** all over the world.*

Affirmatives and negatives

The equipment	is / isn't	made in China.
Smoke signals	are / aren't	used today.

Questions

Is	the equipment	made in China?
Are	smoke signals	used today?

Past simple passive

We form the past simple passive with the past of *be* + the past participle of the main verb.

Use the simple past passive for:

- facts from history.
  *The pyramids **were built** 5,000 years ago.*

- past processes or events.
  *After the battle, the town **was left** empty.*

Affirmatives and negatives

The area	was / wasn't	explored last year.
The caves	were / weren't	discovered in 1850.

Questions

Was	the area	explored last year?
Were	the caves	discovered in 1850?

▶ Exercises 1–4

THE PASSIVE WITH *BY* + AGENT

To say who or what does or did the action (the agent) in a sentence in the passive voice, we use *by*.
*New technology **is developed by scientists** around the world every day.*

However, we don't usually use *by* + agent when the agent is:

- obvious.
  The first Apple iPhone was sold in 2007 (by Apple).

- unimportant.
  Steve Jobs was liked and respected (by everyone in the company).

- unknown.
  My iPhone was stolen. (I don't know who stole it.)

▶ Exercises 5–7

1 Choose the correct option (passive or active) to complete each sentence.

1 Technology *is used* / *used* for exploring the world.
2 Explorers *were made* / *made* the first map of the area last year.
3 I *was given* / *gave* this book last year.
4 *Were you used* / *Did you use* a computer at school?
5 The cave *was discovered* / *discovered* in 2007.
6 He *was found* / *found* an ancient city in the desert.

2 Complete the article using the correct forms of the verbs in brackets.

Genghis Khan (1162–1227) was the most powerful leader in the history of the world, but no one knows exactly where he (1) _____ (bury) when he died. The facts of his death (2) _____ (not know) today either. But explorer Albert Yu-Min Lin (3) _____ (hope) to find out more. In the past, people looking for ancient sites (4) _____ (explore) on foot and often dug a lot of holes. But now, small flying machines with cameras called drones (5) _____ (use) to take pictures from high in the air. These images (6) _____ (study) for signs of ancient buildings. If Lin's team notices something, they (7) _____ (not start) digging immediately. A new technology that can look through stone and earth (8) _____ (use) to 'see' what's underground without digging.

3 Read the article. For each sentence, write *P* (passive) or *A* (active). Then choose the best word to complete the description.

Using technology to explore the world

Every day, new places (1) **are explored** thanks to some amazing technology. Cave diver Alberto Nava (2) **wears** a device called a 'rebreather'. When the diver breathes out, the rebreather (3) **cleans** the air before it (4) **is breathed** again. Rebreathers (5) **are used** when divers want to stay under water for long periods of time and when they want to be very quiet. A rebreather (6) **doesn't make** any bubbles.

1 _____ – the agent is *obvious* / *unknown or unimportant*
2 _____ – the focus of the sentence is on the *subject* / *object*
3 _____ – the *subject* / *object* is the focus of the sentence
4 _____ – the agent is *obvious* / *unknown or unimportant*
5 _____ – the agent is *obvious* / *unknown or unimportant*
6 _____ – the focus of the sentence is on the *subject* / *object*

4 Write questions in the passive.

Present simple:
1 How / the air / switch on

How is the air switched on?

2 Where / the equipment / store
3 What / this machine / use for

Past simple:
4 How many / maps / make
5 When / this photo / take
6 Which / cave / explore

5 Rewrite the paragraph. Put the verbs in bold in the passive and use *by* to show the agent.

Mobile health

In 2011, the Chinese government **started** the Wireless Heart Health project to help rural patients with heart problems. A small wire **connects** patients to a smartphone with equipment that records information about their heart. Then a doctor **checks** the information from the phone, so any advice or a change of medicine can be given if necessary.

6 Read the article. Answer the questions.

3D printing used by doctors to make tools and medical equipment

When Haiti **was hit by a huge earthquake** in 2010, the people needed medical equipment right away. However, sending things to Haiti is slow and **was made almost impossible by the earthquake**. Dara Dotz, who was working to help the people of Haiti, had an idea. A 3D printer **could be used by doctors** in Haiti to make some of the necessary tools and equipment.

1 What is the main focus of each sentence?
2 Which agent isn't necessary?

7 Write complete passive sentences. Add *by* if necessary.

1 Paper / make / wood.

Paper is made from wood.

2 It / first / make / second century / the Chinese.
3 Some parts / the wood / remove.
4 Material / then / wash and dry.
5 Water / take out of it / large machine.
6 Paper / cut into sheets / for printing.
7 It / make / into books, newspapers, etc.
8 Paper products / sell / newsagents and other shopkeepers.

INFINITIVE	PAST SIMPLE	PAST PARTICIPLE
be	was/were	been
become	became	become
begin	began	begun
bring	brought	brought
build	built	built
buy	bought	bought
choose	chose	chosen
come	came	come
cost	cost	cost
do	did	done
drink	drank	drunk
eat	ate	eaten
fall	fell	fallen
feel	felt	felt
find	found	found
fly	flew	flown
forget	forgot	forgotten
get	got	got
give	gave	given
go	went	gone
grow	grew	grown
have	had	had
hear	heard	heard
hurt	hurt	hurt
keep	kept	kept
know	knew	known

INFINITIVE	PAST SIMPLE	PAST PARTICIPLE
leave	left	left
learn	learned	learned
let	let	let
make	made	made
meet	met	met
pay	paid	paid
put	put	put
read	read	read
run	ran	run
say	said	said
see	saw	seen
sell	sold	sold
send	sent	sent
sit	sat	sat
sleep	slept	slept
speak	spoke	spoken
spend	spent	spent
swim	swam	swum
take	took	taken
teach	taught	taught
tell	told	told
think	thought	thought
understand	understood	understood
wake	woke	woken
wear	wore	worn
write	wrote	written

WRITING

UNIT 1 An introductory postcard

Use the person's name to greet them in the salutation (greeting).

Talk about your interests.

End by saying you look forward to hearing from the person and then end with a closing (*Sincerely*, *Best wishes*, *Yours truly*, etc.) and your name.

Introduce yourself and say where you're from.

Ask the person you are writing to about his or her interests.

Hello Thanh,

My name's Timoteo. My friends call me Timo. I'm from Granada, Spain. I'm a student in Year 9.

My favourite subjects are art and music. I love drawing superhero comics, and I play the drums. I'm also really into football. I'm a great player! (But my friends don't always agree!)

What about you? Are you into sports? What are your favourite subjects?

I look forward to hearing from you.

Best wishes,

Timo

UNIT 2 A description (Describing a visit to a house or place)

What is the name of the place? What is it?

How old is it? When was it built?

What was the visit like?

Where is it?

Why is it special? Why do people like it?

Shuri Castle is a brilliant castle in the city I'm from – Naha, Japan. I went there last year when my cousin was visiting from Tokyo, because the castle is famous in our area. The oldest part is about seven hundred years old. It has many beautiful buildings, pretty gardens and huge gates. That's the reason I like it. It's unlike any other place I've ever seen. A king used to live there, but now it is like a museum. When we were taking a tour, the tour guide showed us the inside of the castle and told us about its history. It's definitely the coolest house I've ever seen.

UNIT 3 An opinion essay

Opinion essays will state the argument in the title or in the first paragraph.

Acknowledging other ideas can make your own argument stronger.

Use phrases like *in my opinion* and *for me* to show where you are stating your opinion.

State your own opinion clearly at the beginning of the essay.

Clearly state your opinions and give reasons to support them.

Restate your opinion at the end of the essay.

Agree or disagree: exercising every day is the best way to stay healthy

While it's true that doing a little exercise every day is good for you, I think eating well is more important than exercise.

One reason I think this is that exercise can make people eat too much. Everyone knows someone who exercises and then eats a lot of junk food as a reward. This doesn't improve their health. I believe that for the best health, everyone should first make sure they have a healthy diet.

Second, in my opinion no one should smoke, because cigarettes are bad for you. They're also bad for people around you.

For me, exercise is the third most important thing. It isn't necessary to go to the gym, but you should try to walk to school instead of going by car or bus.

Not smoking and getting exercise are important, but the best way to stay healthy is to have a good diet.

UNIT 4 An enquiry email

Include the name of a person in the salutation if possible. If you don't know the name of the person who will be reading the email, include the name of the company or institution.

Dear City Summer School,

I saw your ad for the two-week course in video-making on vacationcourses.com. I'm writing because I'd like to ask some questions.

First, does each student make a video, or do students work in groups to produce projects? Second, can you tell me if students have to choose to make a story or a documentary, or is it possible to do both?

Thank you in advance for any information you can give me. I look forward to hearing from you.

Yours sincerely,

Alfonso Alongi

Say how you know about the company or course.

Say why you're writing.

End with a polite and professional closing, like *Yours sincerely* or *Best wishes*.

Ask questions about the company or course. Make sure that they show you've done some research.

Thank the person.

UNIT 5 Informal invitations and replies

When you write an invitation, give the time, date, location and type of event. Remember to ask the person to let you know if they can come.

A

Hey Sylvia,

I'm having a birthday party on Saturday the 25th from 5:00 to 10:00 at my house. We're going to have pizza and watch a film. Can you make it?

RSVP

Joanna

B

Hi Davina,

Thanks for inviting me to your graduation party. I'd love to come. What should I wear? Should I bring anything? Let me know ASAP!

Lena

When you accept an invitation, begin by saying thank you. If you have any questions about the event, ask the writer. It can be polite to offer to bring something (food or drinks, for example).

When you say no to an invitation, begin by saying thank you. Apologize that you can't make it, and say why – without giving too many details if you don't want to. It is polite to end by saying you hope they enjoy the event.

C

Anders,

Thank you for the invitation to your New Year's party. I'm sorry, but I can't make it. I've already made other plans.

Lucas

PS I hope you have a great time!

UNIT 6 An advice blog

Sometimes the title of the article will tell you what the problem is.

Look at the first paragraph. The problem, and why it is a problem, should be clearly stated.

The first paragraph should also say how the blog addresses the problem.

Look for each solution. Notice the supporting evidence the author uses. Using supporting evidence helps the author explain how the solution can help somebody.

Dealing with exam stress

It's natural to feel stressed when you have an exam. In fact, if you don't feel at least a little stressed, you probably aren't working hard enough. Stress can help to make us study, but if we have too much stress, it can make us ill and reduce our chances of success. I asked my friends how they deal with exam stress. Here are their top six tips.

No one is perfect. Do your best, but remember: it won't help you to have a lot of stress and worry about getting 100 percent every time.

When you're preparing for an exam, eat well. Your brain needs food! Eat plenty of fresh fruit and vegetables.

If you feel stressed out, talk to another student about it. It helps to remind you that your feelings are normal.

You may want to stay up late studying, but you should get plenty of rest. If you're too tired, you won't learn as well, and you may get ill.

Exercise is one of the best ways to fight stress and clear your mind. When you're planning your exam preparation, you should include regular physical activity.

On exam day, remember to breathe. When you breathe deeply, you feel more relaxed!

If you follow these tips, you'll improve your chances of exam success. Good luck!

The concluding sentence should say what the author thinks will happen if you follow the advice. It might also restate the problem.

UNIT 7 A restaurant review

Make sure to address these points when describing a restaurant.

location

interesting point

recommedation

Freegan Pony, Paris

Place Auguste Baron

Opening hours: Sunday & Thursday 19:30–22:30, Friday & Saturday 19:30–23:00

Freegan Pony is a very welcoming and relaxing place to eat. We went on a Saturday evening, when it was very lively, but everyone was very pleasant and calm.

The brasserie's 'selling point' is that their experienced chefs prepare the meals with imperfect fruit and vegetables – produce that supermarkets don't want, but which is still safe to eat. This is by no means a problem – the food is simple and vegetarian, fresh and tasty.

Of course, one advantage of eating here is that it is cheaper than most restaurants in Paris. You can eat well for less than ten euros.

We would definitely recommend Freegan Pony – it's very good, cheap and it helps the environment. What's not to like?

opening times

atmosphere

kind of food

cost

UNIT 8 A persuasive blog post

State your opinion in the title or at the beginning of the essay.

Introduce your topic with a personal story. It can help people relate to your story and include an example of what you're arguing for.

Clearly state what you want to change.

Mention successful examples of the change you're arguing for.

Making music shouldn't be a crime

When I went to Paris, I enjoyed the performers who played music, did tricks, or painted pictures on the pavement. My town doesn't allow street performers. We should change that.

The world's great cities have street performers: Tokyo, Edinburgh, Barcelona, Mexico City. If we allowed them here, people would come to watch them and would also shop. This would help the local economy.

How did you feel the last time you saw a great street performer? They make a connection with the audience and they make visitors feel welcome.

Some people earn their living this way. It's wrong to stop people from doing honest work. It would be right to change the rules to allow street performers.

If we allowed them, it would improve our quality of life and give entertainers opportunities to perform. Please click on this link to join my campaign.

Explain how what you're arguing for could help people.

Ask readers to think of their own experience and describe the emotional side of your proposal.

Explain what's wrong and what would be right.

End with a call to action that explains exactly what you think people should do.

UNIT 9 A formal email

Include a polite greeting.

Include the reason for writing.

Say who you are. This can help you expand on why you're writing.

Say why you're writing. This can include asking questions.

Use indirect questions to be more polite.

Request a reply if necessary.

End with a polite and formal closing.

Dear Mr Danoff,

My school careers adviser, Ms Wong, has given me your name and said that you can answer some of my questions about user experience design. Thank you very much for this opportunity.

I'm in Year 11 at the Quarry Hill International School. I'm very interested in both art and information technology, and I would like to learn more about being a user experience designer.

I have a few questions.
1 I want to choose some classes related to UX design. Could you tell me what the most useful subjects are? I'm planning to take courses in art, information technology, psychology and design. Do you have other suggestions?
2 Do you know if I need a university degree to work in UX design? If so, could you recommend the best course?
3 I'd like to know if there's a website or magazine that would teach me about the business. I would like to learn as much as I can about what real UX designers do.

Many thanks again for agreeing to answer my questions. I look forward to hearing from you.

Yours sincerely,

Ignacio Suarez

UNIT 10 A formal letter of suggestion

Include a polite greeting.

Explain differences in opinion.

Make a suggestion.

Use specific examples and ideas of how your suggestion would work.

Support your argument.

Thank the person.

Use a polite ending.

Dear Ms Smith,

I'm writing about the new 'no-phones' rule in the cafe area. While I understand that loud telephone conversations are annoying, I don't think quietly sending and receiving texts or checking an app is a problem, especially if phones are put on silent mode. Also, I can see that using a phone while ordering or paying for food is rude to the staff, but when people are sitting alone at a table, texting doesn't bother anyone.

Can I suggest that you replace the 'no-phones' rule with a set of 'use technology politely' rules? For example:

- Think about the people around you.
- Put phones on silent.
- Don't use your phone when you're at the food counter.
- Don't talk on your phone in the cafe area.
- No selfies!

These rules would stop the annoying behaviour but would allow people who aren't bothering anyone to use their devices.

Thank you for considering this suggestion.

Yours sincerely,

Mika Thibeau

UNIT 9 Answers, Vocabulary Exercise 3

1 software engineer
2 electronics engineer
3 nurse
4 doctor
5 accountant
6 high school teacher
7 chef
8 architect
9 dentist
10 lawyer

Source: Business Insider

UNIT 9 Speaking, Exercise 5

Student A
Job: personal trainer
Duties: help people exercise and improve their fitness
Places of work: gym, health club
Necessary skills: good communication, organization, experience coaching
Personal qualities: lots of energy, high level of fitness
Pay: comfortable

Student B
Job: writer
Duties: write and sell books and articles
Places of work: office at home
Necessary skills: writing, good communication, ability to sell work
Personal qualities: able to work alone, able to finish work on time
Pay: very low to very high, depending on success

UNIT 1

active (adj)	/ˈæktɪv/
afraid (adj)	/əˈfreɪd/
angry (adj)	/ˈæŋgri/
anonymously (adv)	/əˈnɒnəməsli/
artful (adj)	/ˈɑːtfəl/
be (v)	/biː/
become (v)	/bɪˈkʌm/
bored (adj)	/bɔːd/
calm (adj)	/kɑːm/
cheerful (adj)	/ˈtʃɪəfəl/
confident (adj)	/ˈkɒnfɪdənt/
cool (adj)	/kuːl/
easy-going (adj)	/ˈiːzigəʊɪŋ/
excited (adj)	/ɪkˈsaɪtɪd/
feel (v)	/fiːl/
friendly (adj)	/ˈfrendli/
frightened (adj)	/ˈfraɪtənd/
funny (adj)	/ˈfʌni/
get (v)	/get/
happy (adj)	/ˈhæpi/
hard-working (adj)	/ˌhɑːdˈwɜːkɪŋ/
helpful (adj)	/ˈhelpfəl/
honest (adj)	/ˈɒnəst/
humanity (n)	/hjuːˈmænɪti/
image (n)	/ˈɪmɪdʒ/
intelligent (adj)	/ɪnˈtelədʒənt/
kind (adj)	/kaɪnd/
language barrier (n)	/ˈlæŋgwɪdʒ ˈbæriə/
lazy (adj)	/ˈleɪzi/
look (v)	/lʊk/
loud (adj)	/laʊd/
nasty (adj)	/ˈnɑːsti/
nervous (adj)	/ˈnɜːvəs/
nice (adj)	/naɪs/
popular (adj)	/ˈpɒpjələ/
proposal (n)	/prəˈpəʊzəl/
quiet (adj)	/ˈkwaɪət/
relaxed (adj)	/rəˈlækst/
seem (v)	/siːm/
serious (adj)	/ˈsɪriəs/
shy (adj)	/ʃaɪ/
smart (adj)	/smɑːt/
sociable (adj)	/ˈsəʊʃəbəl/
soulful (adj)	/ˈsəʊlfəl/
struggle (v)	/ˈstrʌgəl/
talented (adj)	/ˈtæləntɪd/
upset (adj)	/ʌpˈset/
virally (adv)	/ˈvaɪrəli/
worried (adj)	/ˈwʌrɪd/

UNIT 2

accommodation (n)	/əˌkɒməˈdeɪʃən/
bamboo (n)	/bæmˈbuː/
building material (n)	/ˈbɪldɪŋ məˈtɪəriəl/
business (n)	/ˈbɪznəs/
communication (n)	/kəˌmjuːnəˈkeɪʃən/
construction (n)	/kənˈstrʌkʃən/
crowded (adj)	/ˈkraʊdɪd/
designer (n)	/dɪˈzaɪnə/
didn't feel right (phrase)	/ˈdɪdənt fiːl raɪt/
direction (n)	/dɪˈrekʃən/
earthquake-resistant (n)	/ˈɜːθkweɪk rɪˈzɪstənt/
education (n)	/ˌedʒəˈkeɪʃən/
elegant (adj)	/ˈeləgənt/
exploration (n)	/ˌekspləˈreɪʃən/
footprint (n)	/ˈfʊtprɪnt/
historic (adj)	/hɪˈstɒrɪk/
imagination (n)	/ɪˌmædʒəˈneɪʃən/
I've got to tell you (phrase)	/aɪv gɒt ə tel jə/
lively (adj)	/ˈlaɪvli/
location (n)	/ləʊˈkeɪʃən/
make perfect sense (v)	/meɪk ˈpɜːfɪkt sens/
modern (adj)	/ˈmɒdən/
old-fashioned (adj)	/ˌəʊldˈfæʃənd/
residential (adj)	/ˌrezəˈdenʃəl/
rural (adj)	/ˈrʊrəl/
shopping district (n)	/ˈʃɒpɪŋ dɪstrɪkt/
suburban (adj)	/səˈbɜːbən/
sustainable material (n)	/səˈsteɪnəbəl məˈtɪəriəl/
traditional (adj)	/trəˈdɪʃənəl/
transport (v)	/trænsˈpɔːt/
transportation (n)	/ˌtrænspɔːˈteɪʃən/
treat you well (v)	/triːt juː wel/
urban (adj)	/ˈɜːbən/
walkable (adj)	/ˈwɔːkəbl/

UNIT 3

block (v)	/blɒk/
calm (adj)	/kɑːm/
dumb dodo (n)	/dʌm ˈdəʊdəʊ/
frightening (adj)	/ˈfraɪtənɪŋ/
glasses (n)	/ˈglɑːsɪz/
happiness (n)	/ˈhæpɪnəs/
health (n)	/helθ/
healthy (adj)	/ˈhelθi/
hit the books (v)	/hɪt ðə bʊks/
hospital (n)	/ˈhɒspɪtəl/
ignore (v)	/ɪgˈnɔː/
illness (n)	/ˈɪlnəs/
injury (n)	/ˈɪndʒəri/
institution (n)	/ˌɪnstɪˈtuːʃən/
medical (adj)	/ˈmedɪkəl/
medicine (n)	/ˈmedɪsən/
pain (n)	/peɪn/
painful (adj)	/ˈpeɪnfəl/
passed out (v)	/pɑːst aʊt/

patient (n)	/ˈpeɪʃənt/
pseudonym (n)	/ˈsjuːdənɪm/
realize (v)	/ˈrɪəlaɪz/
scary (adj)	/ˈskeəri/
sore (adj)	/sɔː/
specialist (n)	/ˈspeʃəlɪst/
take seriously (v)	/teɪk ˈsɪriəsli/
treatment (n)	/ˈtriːtmənt/
unwell (adj)	/ʌnˈwel/
wrestler (n)	/ˈreslə/

UNIT 4

100 percent (n)	/ˈhʌndrəd pəsent/
applications (n)	/ˌæpləˈkeɪʃənz/
art (n)	/ɑːt/
attend (v)	/əˈtend/
blackboard (n)	/ˈblækbɔːd/
careful (adj)	/ˈkeəfəl/
careless (adj)	/ˈkeələs/
creative (n)	/kriˈeɪtɪv/
desk (n)	/desk/
develop (v)	/dɪˈveləp/
drop out (v)	/drɒp ˈaʊt/
education (n)	/ˌedʒəˈkeɪʃən/
exam (n)	/ɪgˈzæm/
factor (n)	/ˈfæktə/
geography (n)	/dʒiˈɒgrəfi/
go into (v)	/gəʊ ˈɪntuː/
grades (n)	/greɪdz/
gratification (n)	/ˌgrætɪfɪˈkeɪʃən/
hopeful (adj)	/ˈhəʊpfəl/
hopeless (adj)	/ˈhəʊpləs/
in other words (phrase)	/ɪn ˈʌðə wɜːdz/
in trouble (phrase)	/ɪn ˈtrʌbəl/
make it to (v)	/meɪk ɪt tuː/
maths (n)	/mæθs/
notebook (n)	/ˈnəʊtbʊk/
pen (n)	/pen/
primary school (n)	/ˈpraɪməri ˌskuːl/
principles (n)	/ˈprɪnsəpəlz/
private school (n)	/ˈpraɪvət ˌskul/
producing (v)	/prəˈdjuːsɪŋ/
public school (n)	/ˈpʌblɪk ˌskuːl/
science (n)	/ˈsaɪəns/
secondary school (n)	/ˈsekəndəri ˌskuːl/
self-discipline (n)	/ˌselfˈdɪsəplɪn/
skills (n)	/skɪlz/
stress-free (adj)	/stres ˈfriː/
stressful (adj)	/ˈstresfəl/
student (n)	/ˈstjuːdənt/
study (v)	/ˈstʌdi/
take (v)	/teɪk/
teacher (n)	/ˈtiːtʃə/
test (n)	/test/
thankful (adj)	/ˈθæŋkfəl/
useful (adj)	/ˈjuːsfəl/
useless (adj)	/ˈjuːsləs/

UNIT 5

aunt (n)	/ɑ:nt/
best friend (n)	/bes(t) frend/
bonds (n)	/bɒndz/
bow (v)	/baʊ/
brother (n)	/'brʌðə/
central (adj)	/'sentrəl/
classmate (n)	/'klæsmeɪt/
contagious (adj)	/kən'teɪdʒəs/
cousin (n)	/'kʌzən/
cultural (adj)	/'kʌltʃərəl/
emotional (adj)	/ɪ'məʊʃənəl/
family (n)	/'fæmli/
friend of a friend (n)	/frend əv ə frend/
grandfather (n)	/'grænfɑ:ðə/
grandmother (n)	/'grænmʌðə/
historical (adj)	/hɪs'tɒrɪkəl/
hug (v)	/hʌg/
international (adj)	/ˌɪntə'næʃənəl/
kiss (v)	/kɪs/
laughter (n)	/'lɑ:ftə/
musical (adj)	/'mju:zɪkəl/
natural (adj)	/'nætʃərəl/
neighbour (n)	/'neɪbə/
neuroscientist (n)	/njʊrəʊ'saɪəntɪst/
odd (adj)	/ɒd/
origins (n)	/'ɒrɪdʒɪnz/
partner (n)	/'pɑ:tnə/
personal (adj)	/'pɜ:sənəl/
political (adj)	/pə'lɪtɪkəl/
primitive (adj)	/'prɪmətɪv/
professional (adj)	/prə'feʃənəl/
roots (n)	/ru:ts/
say hello (v)	/seɪ heləʊ/
shake hands (v)	/ʃeɪk hændz/
silly (adj)	/'sɪli/
sister (n)	/'sɪstə/
social (adj)	/'səʊʃəl/
stranger (n)	/'streɪndʒə/
teammate (n)	/'ti:m meɪt/
traditional (adj)	/ˌtrə'dɪʃənəl/
typical (adj)	/'tɪpɪkəl/
uncle (n)	/'ʌŋkəl/
vocalize (v)	/'vəʊkəlaɪz/
wave (v)	/weɪv/
weird (adj)	/wɪərd/

UNIT 6

able (adj)	/'eɪbəl/
accept (v)	/ək'sept/
advantage (n)	/əd'vɑ:ntɪdʒ/
agree (v)	/ə'gri:/
appear (v)	/ə'pɪə/
brave (adj)	/breɪv/
bravery (n)	/'breɪvəri/
code (v)	/kəʊd/
comfortable (adj)	/'kʌmftəbəl/
courageous (adj)	/kə'reɪdʒəs/
disadvantage (n)	/ˌdɪsəd'vɑ:ntɪdʒ/

disagree (v)	/ˌdɪsə'gri:/
disappear (v)	/ˌdɪsə'pɪə/
fail (v)	/feɪl/
failure (n)	/'feɪljə/
impatient (adj)	/ɪm'peɪʃənt/
imperfect (adj)	/ɪm'pɜ:fɪkt/
imperfection (n)	/ɪmpər'fekʃən/
impossible (adj)	/ɪm'pɒsəbəl/
inexpensive (adj)	/ɪnɪk'spensɪv/
informal (adj)	/ɪn'fɔ:məl/
negotiate (v)	/nə'gəʊʃɪeɪt/
patient (adj)	/'peɪʃənt/
perfect (adj)	/'pɜ:fɪkt/
perfection (n)	/pər'fekʃən/
perseverance (n)	/ˌpɜ:sə'vɪrəns/
possible (adj)	/'pɒsəbəl/
potential (n)	/pə'tenʃəl/
reject (v)	/rɪ'dʒekt/
socialization (n)	/ˌsəʊʃəlaɪ'zeɪʃən/
socialize (v)	/'səʊʃəlaɪz/
struggling (adj)	/'strʌglɪŋ/
succeed (v)	/sək'si:d/
success (n)	/sək'ses/
support (v)	/sə'pɔ:t/
supportive network (adj)-(n)	/sə'pɔ:tɪv 'netwɜ:k/
trial and error (n)	/ˌtraɪəl ənd 'erə/
unable (adj)	/ʌn'eɪbəl/
uncomfortable	/ʌn'kʌmftəbəl/
unsuccessful (adj)	/ˌʌnsək'sesfəl/

UNIT 7

achievement (n)	/ə'tʃi:vmənt/
appearance (n)	/ə'pɪərəns/
apple (n)	/'æpəl/
bear (v)	/beə/
bitter (adj)	/'bɪtə/
chicken (n)	/'tʃɪkɪn/
chilli powder (n)	/'tʃɪli.paʊdə/
coffee (n)	/'kɒfi/
cosmetic (adj)	/kɒz'metɪk/
corporation (n)	/ˌkɔ:pə'reɪʃən/
curry (n)	/'kʌri/
disappearance (n)	/ˌdɪsə'pɪərəns/
discard (v)	/dɪ'skɑ:d/
drink (n)	/drɪŋk/
farmer (n)	/'fɑ:mə/
flavour (n)	/'fleɪvə/
food (n)	/fu:d/
french fries (n)	/ˌfrentʃ 'fraɪz/
fruit (n)	/fru:t/
global (adj)	/'gləʊbəl/
guacamole (n)	/ˌgwækə'məʊl/
household (n)	/'haʊshəʊld/
hunter (n)	/'hʌntə/
ice cream (n)	/'aɪs ˌkri:m/
invest (v)	/ɪn'vest/
kebab (n)	/kɪ'bæb/
lemon (n)	/'lemən/
lemonade (n)	/ˌlemə'neɪd/
meat (n)	/mi:t/
organism (n)	/'ɔ:gənɪzəm/

pasta (n)	/'pæstə/
pie (n)	/paɪ/
potato crisps (n)	/pə'teɪtəʊ ˌkrɪsps/
prawns (n)	/prɔ:nz/
requirement (n)	/rɪ'kwaɪəmənt/
resources (n)	/'rɪsɔ:sɪz/
salsa (n)	/'sælsə/
salty (adj)	/'sɔ:lti/
scandal (n)	/'skændəl/
snack (n)	/snæk/
sour (adj)	/saʊə/
spice (n)	/spaɪs/
spicy (adj)	/'spaɪsi/
strawberry (n)	/'strɔbəri/
surplus (n)	/'sɜ:pləs/
sweet (adj)	/swi:t/
tackle (v)	/'tækəl/
tea (n)	/ti:/
tomato (n)	/tə'mɑ:təʊ/
traveller (n)	/'trævələ/
vegetable (n)	/'vedʒtəbəl/
worker (n)	/'wɜ:kə/

UNIT 8

advertise (v)	/'ædvətaɪz/
air pollution (n)	/eə pə'luʃən/
ban (n)	/bæn/
be the change (v)	/bi ðə tʃeɪndʒ/
billboard (n)	/'bɪlbɔ:d/
campaign (n)	/kæm'peɪn/
design (v)	/dɪ'zaɪn/
do something about it (v)	/du:'sʌmθɪŋ ə'baʊt ɪt/
go for it (v)	/gəʊ fɔ:r ɪt/
governor (n)	/'gʌvənə/
grow (v)	/grəʊ/
hunger strike (n)	/'hʌŋgə ˌstraɪk/
inspired (v)	/ɪn'spaɪəd/
make that difference (v)	/meɪk ðæt 'dɪfrəns/
manufacture (v)	/ˌmænjə'fæktʃə/
material (n)	/mə'tɪəriəl/
paradise (n)	/'pærədaɪs/
pick (v)	/pɪk/
produce (v)	/prə'dju:s/
rainforest (n)	/'reɪnfɒrɪst/
recycle (v)	/ˌri:'saɪkəl/
recycling program (n)	/ˌri:'saɪklɪŋ 'prəʊgræm/
sealife (n)	/'si:laɪf/
sell (v)	/sel/
shopping bag (n)	/'ʃɒpɪŋ ˌbæg/
throw away (v)	/θrəʊ ə'weɪ/
walk your talk (v)	/wɔ:k jɔ: tɔ:k/

UNIT 9

accountant (n) /əˈkaʊntənt/
agree with (v) /əˈgriː wɪð/
apply for (v) /əˈplaɪ fɔː/
apprenticeship (n) /əˈprentɪsʃɪp/
architect (n) /ˈɑːkɪtekt/
be part of a team (v) /bi pɑːt əv ə tiːm/
break the world record (v) /breɪk ðə wɜːld reˈkɔːd/
chef (n) /ʃef/
(chief) executive (n) /(tʃif) ɪgˈzekjətɪv/
cleaner (n) /ˈkliːnə/
construction worker (n) /kənˈstrʌkʃən ˈwɜːkə/
curiosity (n) /ˌkjʊriˈɒsəti/
decide on (v) /dɪˈsaɪd ɒn/
dentist (n) /ˈdentɪst/
depend on (v) /dɪˈpend ɒn/
do something useful (v) /duːˈsʌmθɪŋ ˈjuːsfəl/
do something you enjoy (v) /duːˈsʌmθɪŋ juː ɪnˈdʒɔɪ/
doctor (n) /ˈdɒktə/
economy (n) /iˈkɒnəmi/
electronic engineer (n) /iˌlekˈtrɒnɪk ˌendʒɪnɪə/
factory worker (n) /ˈfæktri ˈwɜːkə/
finite (adj) /ˈfaɪnaɪt/
firefighter (n) /ˈfaɪəˌfaɪtə/
focus on (v) /ˈfəʊkəs ɒn/
foundation (n) /faʊnˈdeɪʃən/
freedom (n) /ˈfriːdəm/
global (adj) /ˈgləʊbəl/
graduate from (v) /ˈgrædʒueɪt frɒm/
introduce to (v) /ˌɪntrəˈdʒuːs tuː/
lawyer (n) /ˈlɔːjə/
make money (v) /meɪk ˈmʌni/
manager (n) /ˈmænədʒə/
materials (n) /məˈtɪriəlz/
nurse (n) /nɜːs/
office worker (n) /ˈɒfɪs ˈwɜːkə/
paramedic (n) /ˌpærəˈmedɪk/
police officer (n) /pəˈlis ˌɒfɪsə/
reporter (n) /rɪˈpɔːtə/
salesperson (n) /ˈseɪlzˌpɜːsən/
secondary school teacher (n) /ˈsekəndəri ˌskuːl ˈtiːtʃə/
shop manager (n) /ʃɒp ˈmænədʒə/
software developer (n) /ˈsɒftweə dɪveləpə/
tough (adj) /tʌf/
use up (v) /juːz ʌp/
work close to home (v) /wɜː kləʊs tu həʊm/

UNIT 10

achieve (v) /əˈtʃiv/
achievement (n) /əˈtʃivmənt/
achiever (n) /əˈtʃivə/
complex (adj) /ˈkɒmpleks/
control (v) /kənˈtrəʊl/
develop (v) /dɪˈveləp/
developer (n) /dɪˈveləpə/
development (n) /dɪˈveləpmənt/
digital (adj) /ˈdɪdʒɪtəl/
disappoint (v) /ˌdɪsəˈpɔɪnt/
disappointment (n) /ˌdɪsəˈpɔɪntmənt/
discharge (v) /dɪsˈtʃɑːdʒ/
electrodes (n) /iˈlekˌtrəʊdz/
electronic (adj) /elekˈtrɒnɪk/
entertain (v) /entəˈteɪn/
entertainer (n) /entəˈteɪnə/
entertainment (n) /entərˈteɪnmənt/
equip (v) /ɪˈkwɪp/
equipment (n) /ɪˈkwɪpmənt/
improve (v) /ɪmˈpruːv/
improvement (n) /ɪmˈpruːvmənt/
invention (n) /ɪnˈvenʃən/
neurological disorder (n) /ˌnjʊrəˈlɒdʒɪkəl dɪsˈɔːdə/
neuron (n) /ˈnjʊrɒn/
neuroscience (n) /ˈnjʊrəʊˌsaɪəns/
process (n) /ˈprɒses/
progress (n) /ˈprəʊgres/
research (n) /ˈriːsɜːtʃ/
signal (n) /ˈsɪgnəl/
spinal cord (n) /ˌspaɪnəlˈkɔːd/
squeeze (v) /skwiːz/
switch on / off (v) /swɪtʃ ɒn / swɪtʃ ɒf/
technology (n) /tekˈnɒlədʒi/
tools (n) /tuːlz/
try it out (v) /traɪ ɪt aʊt/
volunteer (n) /ˌvɒlənˈtɪə/
weird (adj) /wɪəd/

Perspectives Pre-Intermediate

Lewis Lansford, Daniel Barber, Amanda Jeffries

Publisher: Sherrise Roehr

Publishing Consultant: Karen Spiller

Executive Editor: Sarah Kenney

Development Editors: Brenden Layte, Diane Hall

Director of Global Marketing: Ian Martin

Head of Strategic Marketing: Charlotte Ellis

Product Marketing Manager: Anders Bylund

Director of Content and Media Production: Michael Burggren

Production Manager: Daisy Sosa

Media Researcher: Leila Hishmeh

Manufacturing Manager: Eyvett Davis

Art Director: Brenda Carmichael

Production Management, and Composition: 3CD

Cover Image: Bernardo Galmarini/Alamy Stock Photo

For product information and technology assistance, contact us at
Cengage Learning Customer & Sales Support, cengage.com/contact
For permission to use material from this text or product,
submit all requests online at **cengage.com/permissions**
Further permissions questions can be emailed to
permissionrequest@cengage.com

Student Edition:

ISBN: 978-1-337-27716-7

National Geographic Learning
Cheriton House, North Way,
Andover, Hampshire, SP10 5BE
United Kingdom

National Geographic Learning, a Cengage Learning Company, has a mission to bring the world to the classroom and the classroom to life. With our English language programs, students learn about their world by experiencing it. Through our partnerships with National Geographic and TED Talks, they develop the language and skills they need to be successful global citizens and leaders.

Locate your local office at **international.cengage.com/region**

Visit National Geographic Learning online at **NGL.Cengage.com/ELT**
Visit our corporate website at **www.cengage.com**

Printed in Greece by Bakis SA
Print Number: 01 Print Year: 2017

Paulo Rogerio Rodrigues
Escola Móbile, São Paulo, Brazil

Claudia Colla de Amorim
Escola Móbile, São Paulo, Brazil

Rory Ruddock
Atlantic International Language Center, Hanoi, Vietnam

Carmen Virginia Pérez Cervantes
La Salle, Mexico City, Mexico

Rossana Patricia Zuleta
CIPRODE, Guatemala City, Guatemala

Gloria Stella Quintero Riveros
Universidad Católica de Colombia, Bogotá, Colombia

Mónica Rodriguez Salvo
MAR English Services, Buenos Aires, Argentina

Itana de Almeida Lins
Grupo Educacional Anchieta, Porto Alegre, Brazil

Alma Loya
Colegio de Chihuahua, Chihuahua, Mexico

María Trapero Dávila
Colegio Teresiano, Ciudad Obregon, Mexico

Silvia Kosaruk
Modern School, Lanús, Argentina

Florencia Adami
Dámaso Centeno, Caba, Argentina

Natan Galed Gomez Cartagena
Global English Teaching, Rionegro, Colombia

James Ubriaco
Colégio Santo Agostinho, Belo Horizonte, Brazil

Ryan Manley
The Chinese University of Hong Kong, Shenzhen, China

Silvia Teles
Colégio Cândido Portinari, Salvador, Brazil

María Camila Azuero Gutiérrez
Fundación Centro Electrónico de Idiomas, Bogotá, Colombia

Martha Ramirez
Colegio San Mateo Apostol, Bogotá, Colombia

Beata Polit
XXIII LO Warszawa, Poland

Beata Tomaszewska
V LO Toruń, Poland

Michał Szkudlarek
I LO Brzeg, Poland

Anna Buchowska
I LO Białystok, Poland

Natalia Maćkowiak
one2one, Kosakowo, Poland

Agnieszka Dończyk
one2one, Kosakowo, Poland